Two Mediæval Lives
of
Saint Winefride

Translated by Ronald Pepin & Hugh Feiss, OSB
With an Essay on Winefride's Well-Cult,
by Catherine Hamaker
& an Introduction by Hugh Feiss, OSB

WIPF & STOCK · Eugene, Oregon

Wipf and Stock Publishers
199 W 8th Ave, Suite 3
Eugene, OR 97401

Two Mediaeval Lives of Saint Winefride
With an Essay on Winefride's Well-Cult
By Pepin, Ronald and Feiss, Hugh, OSB
Copyright©2000 Peregrina Publishing Co.
ISBN 13: 978-61097-492-9
Publication date 4/25/2011
Previously published by Peregrina Publishing Co., 2000

CONTENTS

Introduction
  by Hugh Feiss, O.S.B.   7

Robert Pennant's *Life of St. Winefride*
  Translated by Ronald Pepin   27

The Anonymous *Life of St. Winefride*
  Translated by Hugh Feiss, O.S.B.   95

The Well-Cult of St. Winefride
  by Catherine Hamaker   113

ACKNOWLEDGMENTS

We wish to thank M. R. W. C. Holmes, Esther de Waal and Barbara Kline who very kindly provided us with materials which we were unable to locate in our local libraries; Ellen Martin who brought us together; Ellis Peters, who made Saint Winefride a topic of wide interest; Marilyn Hall, our proof-reader; and our publishers and editors at Peregrina who urged us on and provided critical appraisals of our efforts.

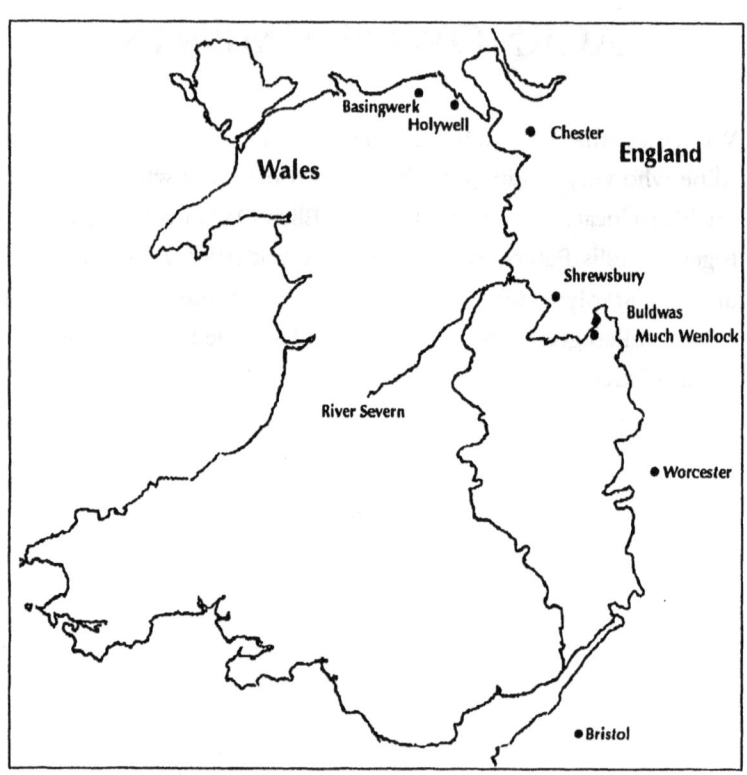

Mediæval Wales

INTRODUCTION

St. Winefride is thought to have lived in seventh-century Wales. Her Welsh name was *Gwenfrewy*, which first occurs in a Welsh text, *Hystoria o Uuched Beuno* (hereafter referred to as *Hystoria*), which can be dated to 1346. The name "Gwenfrewy," was known to Prior Robert Pennant, author of the *Vita et translatio S. Wenefredæ*, who claimed it was a compound of *wen* ("white") and *brewa* (which he said was her original name). In fact, *gwen* can mean both "white" and "holy," while the second member, *"frewy"* is very rare. Whether the Welsh name was transcribed into Latin as *Wenefreda* or the Latin *Wenefreda* transcribed into Welsh as *Gwenfrewy* is not immediately clear.[1]

St. Winefride:
The Physical Evidence

This book presents English translations of two twelfth-century accounts of Winefride's life and miracles, followed by a study of Winefride's spring at Holywell in the context of holy wells in Wales. The origin of one of these accounts and the sources of both are obscure. The surviving physical evidence of Winefride's cult helps dispel some of the obscurity. The physical evidence consists of a fragment from a reliquary; her well, and the associated monasteries of Basingwerk and St. Werburg, Chester; her shrine at the former Benedictine monastery at Shrewsbury; and a finger bone said to be her relic.

Reliquary
The earliest extant object connected with the saint is part of an oak reliquary box. Reports and sketches of this box from the seventeenth

INTRODUCTION

and eighteenth centuries identify the shrine as being triangular in shape, with copper-alloy metal work on the outside with straps for carrying it attached at each end. The reliquary shrine seems to have been influenced by Anglo-Saxon models and to date from the mid-eighth or early ninth century. It was decorated with three metalwork roundels. A surviving fragment of a gable end from the box was acquired by Fr. John Wynne, S.J., from the sexton at Gwytherin church in 1844. In 1858 or 1859 he gave the relic to the church of St. Winefride at Holywell where it has remained. Another fragment came into the hands of Thomas Meyrick, a nineteenth-century biographer of St. Winefride, but that piece seems to be lost.[2]

SITES IN NORTH WALES

Despite Winefride's popularity after her death, few wells appear to have been dedicated to her. The well at Holywell in the far northeast of Wales, however, became an extremely popular pilgrimage place. It is located nine miles from Gwytherin, where she is supposed to have presided over a convent, died and been buried.[3] Some miles to the east, across the border with England, was the Benedictine Abbey of St. Werburg, Chester. In 1119, Earl Richard of Chester confirmed gifts given to this abbey during his lifetime and that of his father. These gifts included "Haliwella," an apparent reference to Holywell. In 1131 monks of the Order of Savigny settled at Basingwerk, about three miles from Winefride's well at Holywell. In 1147–1148 Basingwerk, its founding abbey of Buildwas, and the rest of the Savignac Order were incorporated into the Cistercian Order and Holywell thus became involved in a tug-of-war between St. Werburg's and Basingwerk. At some time during the earldom of Ranulf II (1129–1153), Robert de Pierrepont gave Holywell to Basingwerk. For at least part of the rule of Ranulf's successor, Hugh II (1153–1181), Holywell was back in the hands of the monks of Chester. In 1157 Henry II rebuilt a castle at

≈ INTRODUCTION ≈

Basingwerk which had been destroyed during Stephen's reign and established a house of Templars there to protect pilgrims visiting the well. The Welsh destroyed the castle eight years later. By the end of the twelfth century, Holywell was in Welsh hands again. It was confirmed as belonging to Basingwerk in 1240 by Dafydd ap Llywelyn, prince of Wales.[4] The ties between the monks of Basingwerk and Holywell continued until 1537. In the last half of the fifteenth century Lady Margaret Beaufort (1441–1509) seems to have financed the building of a well chapel and the first publication of a life of St. Winefride.[5]

The Abbey of Sts. Peter and Paul, Shrewsbury

In 1071, Roger de Montgomery was made Earl of Shrewsbury and built castles there and in a number of other places. He also made gifts to churches, founding several in addition to restoring St. Milburga's Priory at Much Wenlock. In Shrewsbury there was a small Saxon church (perhaps originally a collegial or monastic church[6]) dedicated to St. Peter. According to William of Malmesbury, St. Wulfstan of Worcester visited St. Peter's in 1062 and said that although it was insignificant among the churches of Shrewsbury, it would someday be the most glorious church in the region. In 1082, Odelerius, priest of the church of St. Peter, made a pilgrimage to Rome. Inspired by his visit to the basilicas of Sts. Peter and Paul, he urged Roger de Montgomery to establish a Benedictine abbey dedicated to the two saints in Shrewsbury. In March, 1083, Roger vowed to found an abbey on the site of the Saxon church[7] and it was placed in the hands of monks from the Abbey of Sées in Normandy.

In 1087, regular monastic life began under the first abbot, Fulchred of Sées (1087–1119).[8] The original church was 302 feet long and 133 wide, more than ample for a community that seems seldom to have exceeded twenty members during its 450 years of existence. It was

⋄ Introduction ⋄

strategically located on the banks of the River Severn, on a channel which subsequently silted up, and along a main road from London to Wales. The power from the nearby Rea Brook was sufficient to run three mills and provided an important source of income for the abbey, as well as becoming a bone of contention for the townspeople. The monastery had civil jurisdiction over an area called the Foregate and one dependency, the church at Morville, given to it by Roger.

Recent archeology has revealed a great deal about the siting and arrangement of the abbey precincts, although there is still much that remains unknown. Little remains standing, and it is difficult to date and identify what evidence has been uncovered. Excavations are difficult because the surrounding area has been built up and a main road runs through the precincts of the mediæval abbey. On the basis of archeological and written evidence, however, local historians have reconstructed the layout of the mediæval abbey. The church faced to the east, where there was an apse, and beyond that a lady chapel. As was usual, the main (and perhaps only) cloister was fitted into the corner of the south side of the nave and the west side of the south transept. The chapter house seems to have been located in the east range of the cloister, which extended out from the south transept. The abbey wall marking the enclosure went from the north transept around the east end of the church, then south to the Rea Brook, west along this mill brook, then north along the bank of the River Severn, then to the west end of the church. The main entrance to the abbey precincts was just to the west of the west door of the church. South of the mill brook were two fish ponds. Excavations and documentary testimony from the time of the suppression indicate that the abbey was an important provider of hospitality.[9]

In spite of the lofty status of their heavenly and earthly patrons, the monks of Shrewsbury wanted to have the relics of a saint who would serve as an additional patron. One may presume they also hoped that

∽ INTRODUCTION ∽

having relics of a saint would bring pilgrims and encourage donations. The monks of Chester had St. Werburga, the Cluniac monks of Much Wenlock had the relics of St. Milburga, and the monks of Shrewsbury would have the relics of St. Winefride.[10]

In his life of Winefride, Robert Pennant relates how the monks decided to seek her relics. They had heard that there were many bodies of saints in Wales and when one of the monks at Shrewsbury became very ill, the monks of Chester prayed for him. Radulph, who was the subprior, had a dream in which St. Winefride promised that the monk would be cured if the monks celebrated mass at her well at Holywell in Flintshire. And so it happened. The monks of Shrewsbury found her body at Gwytherin in nearby Denbighshire and had the bones taken back to Shrewsbury and kept in the church of St. Giles until, in 1138, the bishop gave permission to take them in solemn procession to the abbey church. Later the monks of Shrewsbury stole the relics of Winefride's mentor, St. Beuno, and laid them in their church with those of Winefride.[11]

RELIC OF A FINGER BONE

In 1540, the monks surrendered the abbey to Henry VIII's commissioners. Six years later, in 1546, the grounds and buildings were sold to speculators, who in turn sold the abbey to William Langley. In this period, just after the dissolution, many of the abbey buildings were stripped or demolished. The nave of the church, which had been used for parochial services, was retained for parish use, but the east end and the transepts were demolished. The shrine to St. Winefride was destroyed and her relics thrown out. It is claimed, however, that one small finger bone was rescued and eventually given to the English College in Rome. One small piece of this bone went to the Roman Catholic cathedral, built in Shrewsbury in 1856, and was then divided: one half went to Holywell, the other was kept at the cathedral.[12] In this

INTRODUCTION

way were Winefride's remains divided between the two places which had kept her memory and her veneration alive for almost 900 years.

ST. WINEFRIDE: THE LATIN LIVES[13]

The story of St. Winefride was told by two twelfth-century Latin authors. There is little question about the authorship or date of the life by Robert Pennant, Prior of Shrewsbury, the *Vita et translatio S. Wenefredae* (here referred to as *VT*, with references to the paragraph numbers of its two parts, indicated as *VT-V* and *VT-T*). There are, however, questions concerning the accuracy of his account. There has been some scholarly debate concerning the author and his origins, and the precise date of the other life, the *Vita S. Wenefrede*, (here referred to as *V* with references to paragraph numbers).

There are extant three manuscripts of Robert's life, dating from the twelfth, thirteenth and seventeenth centuries respectively. Of the anonymous life there is only one extant copy, in a collection of four saints lives written in the early thirteenth century, perhaps at Worcester.[14] The relationship between the two accounts is a scholarly puzzle and in order to understand why, it is necessary to summarise their contents.

THE LIFE AND TRANSLATION OF
ST. WINEFRIDE BY PRIOR ROBERT PENNANT

Prior Robert wrote his *Vita et translatio S. Wenefredae* in or near 1140 and dedicated it to Guarin, prior of Worcester (1124–1142). In his prologue, Robert says he consulted not only documents in the churches of the country in which Winefride lived but venerable and trustworthy priests as well. He gives as his reason for omitting mention of Winefride's journey to Rome and other stories the fact that they were not corroborated by the documents or by trustworthy oral sources.

According to his account, St. Beuno, Winefride's mentor, was led

❧ INTRODUCTION ☙

by divine guidance to seek an abode with Teuyth, the powerful son of a Welsh chieftain. Beuno was well received and began instructing Teuyth's daughter, Winefride, who decided to dedicate her life to Christ. One day, while her parents were at church, she was approached by Caradoc, a man of royal blood, who lusted after her. Stalling him, she fled toward the church but just as she was entering it, her assailant caught up to her. He cut off her head and it rolled into the church. Beuno confronted the arrogant Caradoc, who died and melted away [VT–V 1–7].

Through the prayers of Beuno and the congregation, Winefride was brought back to life but she always had a thin, white scar where her head had been severed. Where her blood had been spilled, a spring endowed with healing powers began to flow. Some of the stones in it retained the stains of her blood and the moss growing in the spring smelled like incense. Many asked to be baptised there. Shortly after these events, Winefride received the veil and before Beuno moved away to the seashore, he made arrangements for Winefride to take over his building. Beuno said she was granted three gifts: the marks of her blood would remain on the stones; those who sought healing from God at the well would be cured; and each year she could send Beuno a gift by simply placing it on the waters which would carry it from the spring to him at his new home [VT–V 8–17].

Winefride gathered a community around her, of which she was mistress, model and eloquent teacher. Beuno died, but records tell of his saintly life, his death and the miracles he performed after his death. After seven years in the place which Beuno had given her, Winefride wanted to move on. She was instructed in prayer to consult Blessed Deifer, who sent her to Saturnus who, in turn, sent her to Elerius. Elerius introduced her into a nearby convent where she succeeded his mother, Theonia, as superior. After a time, Winefride took ill and she died on November 2 or 3. Robert tells us that in his time many people

INTRODUCTION

came to visit the cemetery where she and other holy people such as Elerius, Theonia, Chebius and Senanus were buried. The spring which had sprung forth in the place where her head had been cut off was much admired. More miracles were worked at the spring than at the place of her burial [VT-V 18-40].

In the section of the life devoted to the translation of Winefride's relics, Robert narrates how the monks of Shrewsbury came to secure part of St. Winefride's body. Although they received a favourable hearing from the Bishop of Bangor and the Welsh prince, the people of Gwitherin were won over only gradually. At each step of the way miracles confirmed the rightness of the monks' mission, from overcoming the objections of the local people (a unanimity achieved only by means of a bribe of money to one of them) to finding the body and bringing it to Shrewsbury where the body rested at St. Giles church. More miracles uccrred when the priory was brought to the monastery [VT-T 1-12].

THE ANONYMOUS LIFE OF ST. WINEFRIDE

In comparison to Prior's Robert's account, the anonymous *Vita St. Wenefrede* is shorter, written in a plainer Latin, more graphic, less exhortatory and contains more Welsh names. For the most part, however, the content of the anonymous life is identical with that in Robert Pennant's account except that it recounts a pilgrimage Winefride made from Holywell to Rome and tells of her attendance at a synod. It ends abruptly with her return to Gwytherin, her eloquent teaching to the virgins who joined her there, and her death and burial [V 9].

While Prior Robert's account concludes with the story of the translation of Winefride's relics from Gwytherin to Shrewsbury, the anonymous life ends with accounts of miracles at her well [V 10-29]. The miracle stories are twice as long as the narrative of her life which

≤ INTRODUCTION ≥

precedes them. None of these miraculous events corresponds to those told near the end of the first part of Prior Robert's account (*VT–V* 34-40). As Fiona Winward notes in her excellent study of the two Latin lives, such a collection of miracle stories is unique in Latin saints' lives of Welsh provenance. Winward also identifies some stylistic differences between these miracle stories and the account of Winefride's life [V 1–9]. For example, in the first section Winefride is called *virgo* or *puella*, while in the second she is called *martyr*. The collection of miracle stories may therefore have been joined to the account of the life at some later date.[15]

The miracle stories in this anonymous life seem to be divided, or at least assigned to, political eras in the region: the era when the Danes were subject to the Britons (*V* 10), the time of the French (12), a period of anarchic struggle between the French and the Welsh (13), the time of the French (16), and the time after the expulsion of the French (26). The miracles are also divided into miracles of retribution (10–15), an addendum (28), and miracles of healing (16–27).

THE SOURCES AND RELATIONSHIPS OF THE TWO LIVES

The two lives tell much the same story. Robert asserts that he deliberately omitted the story of Winefride's journey to Rome which begins the last chapter (*V* 9) of the anonymous life which is devoted to Winefride's earthly sojourn. The second half of Robert's work tells of the miracles which accompanied the translation of Winefride's relics to Shrewsbury. Since he wrote shortly after the transferral of the relics, he did not have the opportunity to write at length about the miracles she worked at Shrewsbury. He did observe, however, that by her relics in the abbey church "... cures are granted to the sick, and countless miracles happen for the glory and praise of God." For its part, the anonymous life devotes two thirds of its text to the miracles

Winefride worked at Holywell. It would seem, therefore, that each of these works clearly aimed to tie Winefride's miracle-working power to a specific locale.

The aims of the two authors were not necessarily at odds. If the fame of Winefride's miracle-working prowess grew at one place, it redounded to the glory of the saint's healing powers at the other as well. For example, it is reported that in 1416 Henry V went on pilgrimage from Shrewsbury to Holywell to give thanks for his victories over the French at Agincourt and Harfleur. Both pilgrimage sites seem to have flourished in the late fifteenth century.[16] Moreover, Robert Pennant says that the monks of Shrewsbury would have been satisfied with even a small part of the saint's relics, so some of her bones may have been left at Gwytherin [VT–T 2; but see VT–T 9].

Conjectures about the relationship between the two lives have varied. When they printed the two lives, the Bollandists called the anonymous life the *Vita Prima*. The author of this life makes no mention of the translation of Winefride's bones to Shrewsbury, but instead gave the impression that her remains were still resting in Gwytherin [V 9]. There could be several reasons for this omission. He may have written his life before the translation of the relics or he may not have known about it. Another reason may have been that he deliberately chose to ignore the event entirely. For reasons that will become clear, this third option seems most likely. The author refers to a time after the expulsion of the French (Normans) from Gwynedd [V 25]. As we have seen, the monasteries of Chester and Basingwerk vied for control of Holywell, and their fortunes rose and fell as Normans or Welsh gained the upper hand in the area. There is also the possibility that the part of the anonymous life which is devoted to Winefride's life was written before the account of her posthumous miracles.

As Fiona Winward points out, there must be some relationship

Introduction

between the two lives, since the stories of Winefride's life are so similar. In both accounts, the fountain at the site of her beheading is described as being spattered *(fons scaturivit; fontis scaturigine)* by her blood *(sanguis)* which stained the rocks *(lapides)*, while the moss *(mussa; muscicula)* in the spring smelled like incense *(thus)* [VT–V 13; V 6].

There is considerable evidence that Welsh saints were venerated locally long before the twelfth century and many Welsh saints had a holy well connected with them, a devotion which went back to pre-Christian times. The story of Winefride's decapitation and the restoration of her head, the connection of decapitated saints with wells, and in general a respect for the human head are paralleled in other lives of Welsh saints. The stone which carried the cloak and floated down the river to Beuno may echo ancient Welsh stories of water deities. The stories of the curse which caused Caradoc to melt away and Winefride's pilgrimage to Rome are paralleled in several lives of Welsh saints. It is clear that both of these early Latin accounts of Winefride's life have a connection to Wales.

Furthermore, some of the miracle stories in the second part of the anonymous life have a distinct Welsh flavour. On the one hand, the author of these miracle stories refers to the people in the area of Holywell as *incolae* and *indigenae* ("inhabitants"), suggesting that the author was not a resident, or at least not a native resident, of the area. On the other hand, some of the miracle stories show the saint punishing Normans who encroach on her prerogatives. For example, it is reported that her fountain ran with milk to celebrate the expulsion of the Normans from her territory.

Weighing all the evidence, Winward suggests that the two works draw on a common Welsh source which had been written in Latin. Further, noting the prominence of St. Beuno in the two Latin lives of Winefride, she conjectures that the common source may have been a life of St. Beuno. A clue to that common source may be the Welsh

Introduction

life, *Hystoria o Uuched Beuno* mentioned above in connection with Winefride's name. The *Hystoria* of St. Beuno contains a brief account of Winefride's life and may be a Welsh version of a lost Latin life of St. Beuno. Prior Robert's life contains some details from the story of Winefride's beheading which are found in the *Hystoria*, but not in the anonymous Latin life of Winefride. Robert also says that further information on Beuno's life and death can be found in a respectful account which tells of Beuno's way of life [VT–T 26]. On the other hand, the anonymous life of Winefride contains some information found in Beuno's *Hystoria*, but not in Prior Robert's life; e.g., that the events occurred during the reign of King Cadfan and that Beuno went to Teuyth after being forced to move by the sons of Selym. Finally, the two Latin lives of Winefride have in common some details not found in the Welsh work; e.g., the royal, but not kingly status of Caradoc; Winefride's request to change her clothes; the blood-stained stones and the sweet-smelling incense. Hence, it seems somewhat probable that the authors of our two Latin lives made use of a now lost Latin original of the Welsh life of Beuno, filling out its information on Winefride with legends and stories which were drawn from traditions about her and other Welsh saints, in particular St. Cadocus.

From this evidence, we may conclude that the conjectured Latin life of Beuno was probably written after 1100, since the Latin life of St. Cadocus, with which it has several incidents in common, was written about 1100. Basingwerk was founded in 1131. If the author of the anonymous life of Winefride was a monk of Basingwerk, a Norman living in a Welsh milieu, he probably wrote it at a time when Holywell was in the control of Basingwerk and not under St. Werburg's, Chester. As we have seen, the control of Holywell passed back and forth between the two monasteries, and there may have been times when neither monastery controlled the shrine. The anonymous life of Winefride could have been written at Basingwerk at almost the same

INTRODUCTION

time Prior Robert wrote his life, in order to assert the importance of Winefride's well. However, both the anonymous life and the collection of miracle stories which is included with it could have been written anytime during the last half of the twelfth century. Oddly, it was Prior Robert Pennant's life, not the anonymous life, which had the most influence on later mediæval devotion to Winefride in Wales.[17]

The Latin Texts in the Acta Sanctorum and the Translations

The Bollandists edited the two Latin lives, here translated, in the *Acta sanctorum* for November 3 and prefaced them with a long commentary (pp. 691–701). The anonymous life is called the *Vita prima* (pp. 702–708), while Prior Robert Pennant's *Life and Translation of St. Winefride* is called the *Vita secunda* (pp. 708–731). Following these two lives are the breviary lessons for St. Winefride, as these appeared in the Sarum breviary published in Paris in 1557, and a long appendix regarding holy wells, especially that of St. Winefride. After the Reformation, the Jesuits were particularly active in the area of Holywell. The Bollandists report on the their activities and describe numerous cures reported to have occurred at the well (pp. 731–759).[18]

The translations which follow are based on the texts in the *Acta sanctorum*. The styles of the two Latin texts are quite different. Robert Pennant uses a rather florid style while the anonymous life is written in a rather blunt style. In one sequence of the miracle accounts attached to the anonymous life, their author ends the account of each miracle with a quotation from the psalms. The references are given in brackets in the translation. Accordingly, the two translations are different in style. The translation of Prior Robert's work aims at literal accuracy, so that the syntax of the Latin is evident in the translation. The translation of the anonymous life, while aiming at accuracy,

INTRODUCTION

smooths out the style of the original. One discrepancy in the translations must be noted. In Robert's life, the *"casula"* which Winefride sent down stream to Beuno clearly means "chasuble," a liturgical vestment (*VT–T* 19), while in the anonymous life it seems to have been a secular garment and is therefore translated as "cloak" [V 8].

NOTES

1. Fiona Winward, "The Lives of St. Wenefred (BHL 8847–8851" *Analecta Bollandiana* 117 (1999) 100–103. There are a number of ways to spell the saint's English name. We have chosen "Winefride."

2. Lawrence Butler and James Graham-Campbell, "A Lost Reliquary Casket from Gwytherin, North Wales" *Antiquaries Journal* 70 (1990) 40–48; Nancy Edwards and Tristan Gray Hulse, "A Fragment of a Reliquary Casket from Gwytherin, North Wales" *Antiquaries Journal* 72 (1992) 91–100; Janet Bord, "St. Winefride's Well, Holywell, Clwyd" *Folklore* 105 (1994) 100; Thomas Meyrick, *Life of St. Wenefred, Virgin, Martyr and Abbess, Patroness of North Wales and Shrewsbury* (1878; rpt. Felinfact, Wales: Llanerch Publishers 1996).

3. Hugh Owen and J. B. Blakeway, *History of Shrewsbury* (London: Harding, Lepard and Co., 1825); Roy Fry and Tristan Gray Hulse, "The Other St. Winefride's Wells" *Source: The Holy Wells Journal* n.s. 1 (Autumn, 1994) 18–20.

4. Winward, 94–95, 98. Winward does not mention Adeliza, who according to Fry and Hulse, 18, gave Holywell to St. Werburg's in 1093.

5. Rev. Christopher David, *St. Winefride's Well: A History and Guide* (Privately printed, 1984).

6. Steven Bassett, "Anglo-Saxon Shrewsbury and its Churches" *Midland History* 16 (1991) 13–14.

7. The story of the founding of the Abbey was later retold by

＊ INTRODUCTION ＊

Odelerius' son, Orderic Vitalis. See *Victoria County History of Shropshire*, ed. A. T. Gaydon (London: Oxford Universitiy Press for the Institute of Historical Research, 1973) 2: 30–31.

8. Fulchred was followed by Godfrey of Séez (c. 1119–1128). Orderic Vitalis, who had been a student at the abbey, reported that Abbot Herbert (1128–1138) usurped the office. Under him and his successor, Ralph (1138–1148), Winefride's relics were installed at Shrewsbury. Prior Robert Pennant (later abbot, c. 1150–1168) led the expedition to bring her bones from Wales. In the Br. Cadfael stories, Edith Pargeter (Ellis Peters) depicts Prior Robert as a self-righteous and ambitious man. His life of Winefride shows him to be a self-conscious stylist. For these early abbots see Roy Midmer, *English Mediaeval Monasteries (1066-1540): A Summary* (Athens, GA: University of Georgia Press, 1979) 285; David Knowles, C.N.L. Brooke, and Vera C. M. London, *The Heads of Religious Houses: England and Wales, 940-1216* (Cambridge [Eng]: University Press, 1972) 71; William Dugdale, et. al., *Monasticon anglicanum*. New ed. (London: Longman, 1821) 3: 513–523; Margaret Lewis, *Edith Pargeter: Ellis Peters* (Bridgend, Wales: Seren, 1994) 82–138; Michael Webb, *The Abbots of Shrewsbury* (Privately Printed, 1985; reprinted 1992).

9. For competent summaries of the early history and layout of the abbey, see Nigel Baker, *Shrewsbury Abbey: A Medieval Monastery* (Shrewsbury: Shropshire Books, 1999) 1–14, 20–21, 44–65; Ian Ross, *Shrewsbury Abbey: A Benedictine Foundation; The Parish Church of the Holy Cross* (Much Wenlock: R.J.L Smith, 1999), 3–5. See also, *Current Archaeology*, 109 (1988) 59–62.

10. For Milburga, see Paul Burns, ed., *Butler's Lives of the Saints: February* (Collegeville, MN: Liturgical Press, 1998) 234–235, and for Werburga, Winward, 104, and the literature cited by both.

11. Baker, 7–8; Ross, 5-6.

12. Michael R. W. C. Homes, private communication.

13. We are concerned here with the two earliest surviving Latin lives

of St. Winefride. The Middle English lives of the saint were discussed by Elisa Mangina, "The Saint Who Died Twice: Middle English Lives of Winifred," in a paper delivered at the Thirty-Third International Congress in Medieval Studies, Western Michigan University, Kalamazoo, MI, May 8, 1998. Winward discusses a number of Welsh lives as well as various translations and paraphrases of the Latin lives, most of which were not available to us. We were able to consult Thomas Meyrick's work, cited above, and Herbert Thurston's reprint of Philip Metcalf's *The Life of Saint Winefride* (1712; rpt. London, 1922). For these and other retellings and translations of Winefride's life see Winward, 90, 92.

14. Winward, 89–90.
15. Winward, 115.
16. Baker, 8.
17. Winward, 109–130.
18. For further information on later miracles reportedly worked at Holywell, see C. de Smedt, "Documenta de S. Wenefreda" *Analecta Bollandiana* 6 (1887) 305–352.

The Life of Saint Winefride

by Robert, Prior of Shrewsbury

Translated by Ronald Pepin

Holywell Town

PROLOGUE

*Here begins the Prologue to
the life of Saint Winefride, Virgin and Martyr.*

To His Lord and Father Guarin, the Reverend Prior of Worcester, Robert, his son, a sinner in this life, prior of the monastery of Shrewsbury: may you walk the way of the Lord's commands without stumbling.

One who happens to have learned some small part of the divine benefactions ought, with a pious disposition, to impart charitably to others what has freely been given to him from Heaven for the devotion of those who are one in Christ claims this special mark for itself, namely, to share equally in one knowledge of the faith what each has received from Heaven. In fact, it is a matter of virtue to reveal God's counsels to those desiring them; indeed, it is said to be a matter of constancy and fortitude to report them to those not wanting them or resisting them. But, if someone wished to take unto his own authority what was given for the common use of all, preferring to hide it under a measure rather than supply it for the benefit of others, he would be justly convicted of labouring under the fault of envy for a benefaction brought from Heaven to all wishing it, if at least they are deserving, is considered a duty, and it works to the salvation of all people. Therefore, O Reverend Father, I have not envied you knowledge of the blessings which recently shone forth among us from above, with our friends asking that I make known to you the grace poured forth upon us, not only because in your zeal you have acquired for yourself everlasting renown in the highest degree in offices of this kind, but also because with much prayer you have requested that this be given to you, and, as is reported, you have received what was sent with very great exultation. And since, as a wise man says, every affection is impatient of just and lawful slowness, I am aware that you are sighing with panting breath while you know something is incomplete of those things by which your devotion expects to be made full. Hence, I have just recently sent to you the life of the blessed maiden, Winefride, arranged in order. I assembled it partly through documents in the churches of the country in which she is known to have lived, and partly I learned it from the reports of certain priests whom venerable antiquity commended and whose words their habit of religious life compelled us to trust. First, the fear of God gave me a reason for doing this, lest I be found guilty of having placed the talent entrusted to me in the ground and not lent it out at interest; second, love of the maiden, so that, after her merits were made known, the honour due her might be rendered by the faithful; third, the approval of my brothers, for whose devotion bound firmly to me I have patiently endured so great a labour. For the rest, in that I have been completely silent about her journey to Rome, just as also I have entirely omitted some familiar stories in the mouths of many people - I have done this advisedly, because I did not find these in books nor were those who proclaimed them by their own assertions worthy in the estimation of men whose words I would trust. In truth, it has sufficed for me, and I know it will suffice for you also, that the story of her manner of life be composed in simple language, with all ambiguity removed. Moreover, certain things that were challenged by men who speak truly I have left out lest I be found excessive in words and be found guilty of some superfluity, knowing that these words can suffice for discerning the life of this most holy maiden, and likewise believing that with her assistance and the assent of your prayer I shall obtain from God the reward of my labour.

THE LIFE OF SAINT WINEFRIDE, VIRGIN AND MARTYR.

1

In the western district of Great Britain there is a certain province called Wales, bordered on one side by the territories of the kingdom of Anglia and, on the other side, by the Ocean sea. This land was once inhabited by holy people of many diverse merits and even to this day, it is much honoured because of their countless prerogatives. From their number, a certain illustrious saint still remains eminent, Beuno by name, a most excellent man and chief among that entire multitude of saints. And so when he had first disdained his father's land and scorning the glory of the world and spurning its pernicious enticements, he fled as a pauper and became a monk, living the life of a perfect man in Christ. After he had built churches in various places and appointed brothers to serve God in them, he was urged on by a divine utterance and went elsewhere to seek a dwelling shown beforehand to him by God. With the Holy Spirit truly guiding him and directing his steps for the benefit of many, he came to the manor of a certain great and very powerful man by the name of Teuyth, who was the son of a mighty, excellent chieftain, Eylud by name, one second only to the king. Teuyth disdained to allow anything inconsistent with his own lineage or which might dishonour so great a family, but he followed the nobleness of his family with upright morals and showed himself to be outstanding in every grace.

2

Thus when the venerable man, Beuno, had come to him, he was received by him kindly enough and reverently. Not delaying for long what he was pondering in his mind to disclose, and wishing to make known the reason for his coming, when he had been summoned privately, Beuno said: "Lord, subject to a heavenly inspiration, I have been sent to you. For although up to now I have lived in diverse places and found dwellings suited to my plan and sufficiently agreeable to my purpose, yet nowhere has my spirit been able to rest, with the Spirit of the Lord secretly admonishing me to look for another place. Hence, with those dwellings left behind which to me were very pleasing, to you have I come, not knowing why Divine Providence which presages future events has directed me here. Indeed, I think that it has not happened by chance or without a reason for the certain mystery, since I have believed without hesitation that all things are done by the will of God alone, and the plans of man are always carried out under God's direction. Therefore, if you give assent to my wishes, it will be of importance to your care for yourself to make my coming work for your salvation, and to direct your thoughts patiently to my requests, and to devote the understanding of your mind effectively to them. And so I pray that you consign to God and to me a part of the property distributed to you by lawful inheritance from your ancestors so that I might there build a church, in it to serve God and to offer prayers every day for your salvation.

3

Then, Teuyth, who had now decided to submit with his whole heart to the will of Beuno, since he judged him to be a man worthy of praise and one to be held in reverence, answered him in words of this kind: "It is right indeed to grant to this man a part of these lands which were bestowed upon us by God, and to return acceptable thanks according to our capacity for His favours to us. For you, who seek from me that which I much rejoice to give and which I am not unaware accrues to my own good, make yourself pleasing to me. Therefore, come and take what you ask, namely this country estate, free and clear and exempt from all which pertains to me or my successors, from this day forward transferred to the service of God alone. And since I have an only daughter in whom rests almost the whole of my joy and my hope of posterity, entrusting her to you, I pray that you intercede with the Lord for her so that He might incline her will to His own and her manner of life to my honour, and He might increase my joy from her." Saying these words, he handed over to the blessed man that manor on which to build a church and construct dwellings for the servants of God to stay therein. In fact, transferring all his own goods to another place, he fixed his abode opposite, from which place at every hour of the day he could watch the dwellings of the holy man. Thus in a short time the holy man had conquered the spirit of Teuyth, so that if ever he was torn away from necessary conversation, it seemed to him agreeable and pleasing to direct his sight to that place to which he inclined with the desire of his mind, and to visit with his bodily vision the place where he dwelt in the devotion of his soul.

4

Indeed, when the saint attended to constructing his church, he sometimes put his own hands to the task, always sufficiently managing the expenses and hastening the work by his own toil and industry. Sometimes when the blessed man would celebrate the divine mysteries, Teuyth was present with his wife and daughter, Winefride by name. Moreover, if ever the holy man was revealing the precepts of God to the people, Teuyth placed the aforementioned maiden at the feet of the man of God, admonishing her to pay attention wisely to all of them, and to receive with an open heart what was being said by him. God, foreknowing future events, did not allow this to happen in vain. For the maiden, about to become a temple of God, received with ardent longing what she heard with her ears and stored it in her tenacious memory, soon to show in her works what then she was heaping up in her mind. Often, too, when leave had been asked and obtained from her parents, she came to the man of God, drinking in with a thirsty heart the words which were brought forth from his mellifluous mouth. And although she was loved tenderly by her parents, and the hope of increasing their offspring and the succession of their posterity depended on her alone, yet they considered it a pleasing thing that she was glad to visit the holy man, wishing her to be taught by his discourses to renounce every impure union and to keep herself undefiled for marriage. She, moreover, through the mercy of God inwardly inspiring her, increased daily in goodness and advanced in wisdom, her soul fervently inflamed by the Holy Spirit. Then she determined to renounce utterly every man, and she intended to long for the embraces of God alone, but she was afraid for this to become known to her parents. She believed that it would not be right for her to displease them, but she understood that it was salvific to be united entirely to the true God. She knew the will of her parents in this matter to be harmonious and consistent, so that, lawfully given in marriage to a man, she might keep up the propagation of their offspring; but yet, she believed surely that it would be much better to offer herself as a pure virgin to Christ.

5

Therefore in this spiritual struggle, the maiden's mind was distracted by much tortuous turning, on this side by fear of her parents drawing her away from her intention, on that side by love of God driving her to carry out quickly what she had conceived in her mind. She had been taught by her master to place trust in the words of the Lord, her teacher, to renounce her father and mother, and to follow Christ, but her tender, immature age was an impediment. Yet she decided and firmly fixed in her mind to do that at last, if she could not otherwise gain what she intended. However, she considered it proper first to address her parents through the blessed man and, with the grace of God helping, to make them agree with her. Thus, coming to him, she found him devoting himself to his accustomed prayer, and boldly rushing forth into his presence, she made him aware of her secret. She said: "I want it to be clear to you how much the seeds of the divine word poured out for me from your mouth have increased their yield in me. I have chosen to reject all the excess of the world, and I have determined to preserve my virginity intact and undefiled in honour of the heavenly bridegroom, and this, O most holy Father, I beg that you obtain for me from my parents by your aid."

6

Hearing these words, the saint, moved by her piety and rejoicing that now the divine seed was sprouting in her, said that he would eagerly address her parents and bring about as best he could that which she asked. This was very easy to do and not difficult to obtain, not only because the parents of this maiden had placed themselves entirely under the protection of him who was brought in to intercede, but also because the fullness of divine nectar had imbued their spirits, by which they strongly wished all men to be inebriated, especially the soul of their daughter. Therefore, when they had learned the ardent wish of the daughter from the man of God, drenched by tears, they blessed God and freely granted what was requested, invoking divine assistance for her. Thus, with the burden set aside by which they were greatly weighed down, they divided the wealth of their possessions in various ways to the poor, administering aid to the widows and orphans, and being carefully attentive to the servant of God. And since they saw their daughter willing to be given in marriage to no one except the Son of God, gathering all the things which they were keeping to be bestowed on him if she were to wed an earthly husband, they spent these on divine services. Also, freed from the cares oppressing them so much up to then, they subjected themselves entirely to the precepts of God, following unswervingly the way of justice.

7

Indeed, when the girl had obtained her earnest wish, she was moved by great joy, and, exulting in the Holy Spirit, she sometimes sat as a votary at the feet of the blessed man, drinking in with a thirsty heart the words about the glory of her betrothed which flowed from his mouth. And when freedom was granted her to use her own authority, with a full heart she hastened on the path of God's commandments, always advancing forward and leaving entirely what was behind. For love of Him to Whom she had devoted herself, she admitted nothing earthly into herself, longing with the prophet for One Alone, namely, to dwell in the house of the Lord all the days of her life. Now she did not await the arrival of her parents at church, but sometimes making her way there hurriedly herself, she attended the divine mysteries; moreover, she often kept watch in the church at night. Sometimes even besetting the holy man, she urged him to make a sermon and to discuss the ways and the life of her betrothed. In fact, although entirely inflamed by longing for Him, she then had some joy when she heard him speak of the excellence, the glory and the power of her Friend. Refreshment of this kind surpassed for her every enjoyment of earthly possessions and in her heart, she kept the unfailing delight of spiritual enjoyment. And although she was young in age, yet she was mature in morals and venerable at heart, having a spirit which despised all passionate desire. Certainly, whatever of consummate virtue it is fitting for a man to have was found abundantly enough in her, and the fullness of divine grace had poured the whole sufficiently into her. In outward appearances also, she had received much favour from God, for she was very fair of face and affable in speech and very seemly in her whole body. For this reason, she was not able to avoid always the subtlety of the cunning ambusher, for from this an occasion arose when she was forced to do battle with the Enemy of the human race. For since she was very zealously watchful in the exercises that concern salvation, the devil, seeing that many losses of his power might occur through her and that his strength could be weakened in that country, began to rise up wholly against her and to exert his might. He did not cease until he thought that he had defeated her and that she could not harm him further. The beginning of this was as follows.

8

After the blessed Beuno had finished the building of his church with God's help and had consecrated it to God, the neighbouring people used to come often to it, but almost every day the parents of the aforementioned maiden came there to hear what were the words of God. Moreover, it happened on a certain Sunday, with all the people proceeding to church, that the parents of the maiden also went there so that they might be present at the preaching of the holy man and at the celebration of Mass. However, the maiden, their daughter, perhaps having suffered some ailment, was compelled of necessity to remain at home alone. Behold, a certain youth named Caradoc, the son of King Alan, on entering the house came upon the maiden sitting alone near the hearth. When she saw the king's son, she arose immediately, asking humbly what his purpose was. Indeed, when he inquired where her father had gone and said that he wanted very much to speak with him, the girl responded and said: "Wishing to be present at the divine mysteries, my father has gone to church, and so if he is needed by you, you must wait a little for him to return here." Saying these words with an innocent mind, she suspected no guile or subtlety or any trick. However, in fact, the incentives of lust prompted him and titillated his mind; completely unrestrained, he flew headlong to satisfy this lust, for when the girl had said that he must wait for her father, the youth answered: "I shall patiently await his arrival if you, meanwhile, become my friend and submit to my desire. You know that I am the son of a king, full of riches and many honours; I shall enrich you abundantly if you are willing to agree to my request." Indeed, knowing that he was speaking about copulation, with downcast look and blushing with shame, she pretended that she was indeed chagrined because he had found her unkempt and unadorned. Then she said to him: "Since you, born of royal stock, will soon be a king, God willing, I do not doubt that I should be richly filled with worldly happiness joined in marriage to you. However, be patient a little while until my father arrives, and I, meanwhile, will go into my bedroom and shall return to you quickly." Saying these words, she was really seeking only to be separated from him for an hour. In fact, she saw that he was a very wretched man, inflamed by unfortunate lust, mortally tormented by love of her, and that he had become almost frantic. She also knew that this dangerous enemy was made more insane by her parents' absence, and so she intended to be removed immediately from his grasp by any pretext. In the end he allowed her to go to her room, expecting that she would return to him without delay and more acceptably adorned with seemlier attire. Then she arose and entered her bedroom; without lingering, she went out through the door of her room on the other side, and with swift flight made her way toward the church. For there she thought she would be protected and defended, if not by his fear of God, at least by the crowd of people.

9

This flight soon was known to the unfortunate youth, who immediately became enraged and filled with violent anger because she fled so as not to be united to him; grasping his sword, he swiftly began to pursue her. And since a little distance separated her father's house from the church, he caught up to her with little effort. He first looked at her with a savage expression and then addressed her with these words: "Once I loved you and wanted to embrace you. Now you flee one who comes to you and despise one who seeks you. Then, know for certain that either you will be united voluntarily to me right away, or you will end your life without delay when your head has been cut off by this sword."

The maiden turned her eyes toward the church and anxiously watched if anyone might come from there who would bring her aid, but no one came forth straightaway. Then she turned to the youth and said: "Joined in matrimony to the son of the eternal king and judge of all men, I can accept no other. And lest I detain you longer, I shall admit no one except him while I live, for this could not happen without affront to him. Therefore, draw your sword, put forth your strength, readily use any ferocity you please. Be certain that neither your terrors nor enticements nor promises nor threats can tear me away from the sweetness of that love to whose embraces I am already bound and to whose devotion I am joined." When the impure youth heard himself so defied, he was unable to bear his lust and, at the same time, believing that she could not be weakened and that he could have no peace while the maiden lived, he cut off her head with his drawn sword. As soon as the head of the maiden fell to the ground, a most clear spring burst forth in that very spot and spread itself copiously, offering health to many sick people through the merits of the holy maiden, which even today has not ceased to flow. Since he had seized the maiden near the door of the church and there had severed her head, her body remained outside the church, while the head immediately tumbled into the church, for the church was situated at the foot of a certain slope, and it was on the descent of that mountain that the head of the maiden was cut off, and when it tumbled down, it rolled easily into the church, while her mutilated body remained at the spot where it had first fallen.

10

In truth, when the head tumbled among the feet of the people who were standing in the church and attending the divine mysteries, everyone present was greatly astonished. They were all filled with great fear and said that since an abominable sin had been committed, it must be harshly punished. While they were denouncing the perpetrator, the girl's parents who had been roused by the excitement of the others, approached to learn more surely the reason. When they saw their lifeless daughter and looked at her severed head in one place and her mutilated body in another, they fell to the ground weeping and, consumed by sorrow and anguish, they uttered a lamentable cry and poured forth their grief in wailing cries. When the great commotion arose in the church with all the people lamenting the maiden's death and with many of them filled with great pity at the bitterness of grief which had overcome her parents, the saint heard the din and suspected strife and he came to the crowd of standers-by. When he saw the maiden whom he had consecrated to God so cruelly slain, he was mournfully distressed. Indeed, the murderer was still standing there arrogantly next to the lifeless body and was cleaning his sword, dripping with the maiden's blood on the grass with all the people looking on. Since he was a king's son, he thought that he had perpetrated so shameful an act with impunity, but also, by admitting such a great outrage, he also showed that he did not fear God at all. The saint bore with displeasure his arrogance and hardness of heart and his open boasting of the commission of this crime and he approached him, holding held the head of the maiden in his hands. Looking the youth in the face, he began to address him with these words: "O wicked one," he said, "with a murderous crime defiling the nature of your youthful beauty and the lineage of your royal dignity, why does it not grieve you to have admitted so great a crime? You have confounded the peace and polluted the church by your sacrilege, and impiously provoked God, and yet you are not sorry. Now, moreover, since you have not spared the church nor shown respect for the Lord's day, I beseech my God that you now receive fitting recompense for what you have shamefully committed." When these words had been spoken, the youth instantly fell to the ground and died. And wondrous to say, in the sight of all standing there, the body of the dead youth melted and disappeared and many people affirmed that it had been swallowed up by the gaping earth and had sunk with his soul into the abyss. Indeed, all seeing this were struck with unspeakable fear due to the strangeness of this unaccustomed portent.

II

Then, often kissing the head of the maiden which he held in his hands, the saint was troubled in spirit and compelled to weep. Afterwards he arranged the head and brought it to the rest of the body and, spreading his cloak over it, he breathed into the nostrils. Then he ordered the parents, who were giving no room to consolation but were lamenting their daughter's death with continuous weeping, to pause in their mourning and to cease from their sorrow. He then approached the altar to celebrate Mass and when this was finished, with all the people turning to him and raising their hopes to God, he went to the lifeless body. There he made a splendid sermon for the people, saying, among other things, that the blessed maiden had made a vow to God but that, prevented by death, she had not had enough time for fulfilling it; and, therefore, prostrating themselves devoutly on the ground, they ought to implore God for her resurrection, knowing that they would receive many blessings through her in the future. This they did with care, and they pitied the girl's untimely death and the parents' wretched misfortune. Thus, after they had prayed a long time, rising from the ground and stretching his hands toward heaven, the blessed man said: "Lord, Jesus Christ, for whose love this maiden spurned earthly things and desired heavenly ones, in your mercy hear us calling upon You with devout souls, and pour forth upon us the bowels of your compassion, making Yourself now the perfector of our wishes. And although we are aware that this maiden, having suffered for Your love, now in the bosom of heavenly joy, has no need of our fellowship any longer, yet You, Most Merciful Father, showing Yourself beneficent and ready to hearken to Your sons who pray to You, offer Your assent to their supplicatons. Therefore, command that the soul of this girl brought back to her body might prove that You have rule and domination over souls just as over bodies so that, by the grace of Your mercy, alive again, she might praise Your name; and after a long span of life, with the interest multiplied on her manner of living, she might return to You, her betrothed, in truth the only Son of God the Father, with Whom and the Holy Spirit, You live and are in glory, God, forever and ever."

12

When all had responded "Amen," the girl arose as if from sleep, and, wiping off her face and cleansing it of dust and sweat, she filled those standing by with astonishment and joy. Henceforth, where her head had first been severed along the neck, and afterward by divine power it had been attached and reunited, a certain very slender whiteness, like a thread, surrounded her neck and covered the place of the cutting. Thereafter, this always remained this way as long as the maiden lived in the body to indicate the severing of her head and the proof of a miracle. They say that from that time, people of that province called her Winefride, when before, as they affirm, she was named Brewa. For what those people call "Wen" in their tongue, they call "candidum" (white) in Latin, and so, on account of the whiteness encircling her neck, she is said to have her name from this. With the particle "Wen" added, and with two letters of her former name shifted for the sake of euphony, a word is constructed to obtain the name which is called "Winefride." It is even said that after she had departed from this world, she appeared openly to no one at all who did not see her neck encircled by that white mark. By this evidence, she indicates that the sign of her suffering pleases her still, which she shows clearly as often as she manifests herself to anyone.

13

In truth, the place where her blood was shed used to be called Dry Vale originally, but after the severed head of the maiden had touched the ground and, as we said before, a spring of gushing water arose there which flows even to the present day healing all illnesses both among people and among cattle, this very place has taken its name from the name of the girl. For "Fennan Winefride" in their tongue is rendered "Winefride's spring" in ours and "Fennan" signifies "fons" in the Latin language. And since much blood had poured forth from her body lying on the descent of the sloping mountain, stones tinged by its spattering were lying here and there both in the gushing waters of the spring and in the stream or on the edge of both. And, a marvel to say and to hear, those stones spattered with blood still retain that original spattering, as is well known even today to those wanting to know. For they are stained as if by the congealed blood, nor are they wiped clean by the mold of time nor by the constant washing of the water flowing past. In fact, the moss which clings to these same stones smells like incense. It is acclaimed enough and very well known to the inhabitants of that country that the spring still continues in the original way, and the stones in it, as we said before, are found to be stained with blood, clearly manifesting the merits of the maiden and bringing hope to all that this same maiden can aid those calling upon her. Indeed, the people of that province who had not yet known God nor understood His justice, seeing the raising of the maiden from the dead, and seeing that so clear and evident a miracle had been performed in the flowing forth of the spring and in the spattering of the rocks, prostrated themselves at the feet of blessed Beuno and asked that they be initiated in the mysteries of God. Receiving them with kindly devotion, he purified them with the water of holy baptism and, when they had been instructed by his discourses upon divine precepts, he confirmed them in the service of God.

14

Now we shall take care to tell concisely how, in fact, the blessed maiden Winefride lived after her rising up from the dead, for instance, what manner of life she had, or to what end she came when the course of this present life was finished. When, therefore, she had risen from the dead, as we said before, clinging to the feet of the saintly man for the whole day, she listened with unremitting devotion to his discourses, wishing to be fully instructed about all things which pertain to God. When this had been done and the tenets of church teaching were understood, she ran to the feet of her teacher and resolutely asked to receive the veil. "Since," she said, "this has been granted to me by my parents, and since you know that my soul, despising every worldly excess, longs for the love and acquaintance of God alone, there ought to be no delay, but the solemn obligations of my ardent desire should be followed. Certainly, in no way shall I be able to be dragged from You or pulled away from your feet before, initiated with your blessing into the mysteries of regular discipline, I shall have shown even by my outer appearance that I am of the religious life. Therefore, Holy Father, do not defer for long my ardent desire, but, giving assent to my entreaties, bring it about that I obtain my wish." Then, when her parents had been summoned, the blessed man made known the will and wish of the maiden, and he said that divine grace had first been called upon her, and he announced that he was willing to satisfy her desire. In fact, with her parents kindly consenting and embracing their daughter's vow with an agreeable disposition, the saint consecrated her in her holy veil before many people and confirmed her fully in the disciplines of the regular way of life. Immediately after the vow of her ardent desire had been fulfilled, undertaking the practice of every virtue and engaging most devoutly in studies of the regular discipline, in a short time she acquired knowledge of the whole order and perfection in its observance. Henceforth, advancing more and more each day, she made the blessed man very glad on account of her great charity.

15

After her parents had been summoned, he made a speech of this kind: "You," he said, "received me here in former times and showed yourselves prepared for and disposed to my requests. Then you also granted this place to be established for the service of God, and you strove to complete it effectually. Now, indeed, since divine blessings abound in your midst, earnestly give heed to the heavenly light poured upon you and your daughter, and, considering carefully the grace with which you are sprinkled, take care to walk vigilantly on the path of salvation shown to you. And since you are now about to be without my presence, because God calls me elsewhere, wisely regard the examples and admonitions of your daughter, knowing most certainly that she will be a model not only for you but, in truth, even for all people." Indeed, when he had turned toward the maiden, he said, "God commands you to succeed to my labours and duties, and to live in these dwellings, and to walk without ceasing on the path of life mentioned before to you by me, and to show the path to be traveled to others. For He orders you to bear the palm of singular merit before Him, and by the example of your martyrdom and your profession of a good life, He has determined that many in this world should be instructed in His love. Therefore, from now on it will be your place to dwell in, and to gather virgins who will excel in the service of God and who will remain here with you. And you may know one thing for certain: you will not end your life in this place, for when you have spent seven years here serving God in continual fasting of the body and affliction of the soul, it will be necessary for you, urged on by divine providence, to look for another place, with God guiding you and, through you, illuminating the shadows of many hearts. Again, remember this, because your memory will be renowned in this world, and as much as you will have merit with God, many people will bear witness that they have obtained cures for their infirmities through you."

16

And while the blessed maiden was weeping, much saddened over the departure and absence of her teacher, Blessed Beuno took her right hand and led her to the spring which we pointed out above had flowed forth from the place where her severed head had fallen. Stationing her on one stone which then, by chance, was found there, and even today remains in the stream of the spring and is called "Saint Beuno's stone" by the inhabitants of the place, he addressed her once again with these words: "Here," he said, "you still see the traces of your suffering. Behold, those stones spattered by your blood show that you suffered martyrdom for God, and to your everlasting honour and as a memorial for many others, they preserve, as if fresh, that spattering which wet them with your blood. Now, therefore, in a diligent and retentive memory, store away my words, which will come to the notice of many people by your reverent reporting, and which will much benefit some people through the succession of time to come. Understand that three gifts have been given to you by God which will solemnly proclaim the reason for your praise, and which will increase through proper veneration the love of your devotion in the minds of future generations. In truth, the first is that these stones drenched by the sprinkling of your blood will not be able to be cleansed through the ages by any washing nor to be washed off by the constant, swift motion of the water, but, always bloodstained, they will be visible as a manifestation of your suffering, with God working such a miracle for the glory of His own majesty and as a triumphant sign of your chastity. Indeed, the second gift is that whoever has suffered some misfortune and sought you and asked to be freed from his illness or oppression through you, will rejoice that he has gotten what he asked for when he has been granted his wish the first or second or surely the third time. Moreover, if it happens that one petitioning you has not obtained what he wanted by the third request, let him know most certainly that he will be deprived of the light of the present life soon, and so through the hidden judgment of God he has at present lost the fruit of his prayer. Yet, let him understand that to have called upon you constantly benefits him for the healing of his soul, and through you something greater is divinely given to him than if he obtained outwardly what he requested. Moreover, the third gift is of this kind: When I shall have departed from you shortly, God will deign to bestow on me a suitable place to stay on the seashore. Although I shall be separated from you by a great distance, yet the Most High commands that I be visited every year by your gifts. Therefore, when you have ready in your hands what you wish to send to me, hurry with your gift to this spring here before you and, whatever it will be, entrusted first to God, place it confidently in the spring. Immediately you will see what you have deposited there carried by divine power from the spring through the stream, and, by the force of the running water, conducted unharmed beneath the great, flowing river. And soon, with the wave of the sea submitting to God's will and offering its service, what you have placed in the spring will be carried to the door of my little lodging, carried unharmed over the winding currents of waters, over the swelling, roaring storms of the sea right to my dwelling. With God commanding it, this will also have to happen for all the years that I shall be a sharer in this life. These three gifts, significant of the privilege divinely conferred on you, will be granted to you by God, and while this world lasts, they will be extolled in the reports of many people for the celebration of your memory and the glory of your praise." When these words had been spoken, he led her back to the church, addressing her again in words of this kind: "Behold, this church and the dwellings standing around it, built partly through my toil, partly through the expenses of your parents, I leave to you so that, since I am leaving here, when many virgins have been assembled who will remain with you in the service of God, you might serve God here according to your purpose, never neglecting the good way of life and the examples of living recommended to you by me. And know that in this place there will be a great manifestation of divine power for the benefit of many, and through the example of those remaining here many people will grow in the knowledge of God; they will denounce all the profits of the world so that they might gain Christ. Also, various healings of souls and bodies will be granted here at random to people sick with diverse infirmities; indeed, every age or sex will rejoice that it has attained some remedy in this place. But also I declare that not even brute animals will be lacking in the benefits of this place, with God protecting this dwelling by His merciful might and performing such great signs in it for the celebration of your glory. You, show yourself so truly acceptable to God and make yourself so excellent in all things that in you His holy name might live in glory, and you might become a model of salvation to those who look to you. But now I depart from here to serve God elsewhere according to my custom, and to keep your devotion in sweet remembrance within the recesses of my heart while I live."

17

Saying these words, he started to go away after he had taken up his staff alone, leaving everything to the blessed maiden and her comrades, all the furniture of his house and whatever God had given to him through the hands of the faithful while he was living there. And so, when all had been commended to God and farewell had been said to all, he departed, content with only one cleric as his companion, and he was turning his eyes ever toward blessed Winefride, his cheeks wet with many tears on account of her bodily absence. Indeed, distraught over his words and his departure, saying that she was left without an adviser, exposed to all the attacks of enemies, and forsaken by the presence and attentiveness of her pastor, she had a face sad with tears and sorrow. Although many people tried with comforting words to soothe her while she was escorting her father for a time as he was leaving from the church, she accepted no consolation at all while she was with him. Truly, not one of her companions walking along the way with her could keep from tears, seeing her tormented by such bitter grief. In fact, enduring her weeping no longer and wishing to put an end to so much lamentation, although he was moved by great pity, the saint was separated from her by his swift pace, after his hand had first been extended and a blessing bestowed. Yet, she followed him with anxious glances, and when he was no longer visible, the maiden returned with her companions to her house. Still, she was by no means able to conceal the bitterness of sorrow which had assailed her on account of the departure of her teacher as long as his memory was fresh.

18

Moreover, after a little time had passed, returning to herself and calling to mind again the manner of her conversion, and the glory of her suffering, and the sermons of blessed Beuno her teacher, or his prophecies, she set aside all her grief completely, undertaking a vigorous constancy and immediately, with all the love of her soul, embracing Christ, her betrothed, to Whom she had devoted herself by living chastely; she began to long for Him, to know Him, to sigh for Him with burning desire. Then, gathering the daughters of noblemen to herself, she taught them to love chastity, and with all the enticements of this alluring world rejected, to submit their necks to the light yoke of Christ, and to give themselves up to the service of God through the rule of the monastic life. Some, moreover, observing the severity of that manner of life and the moral seriousness of the life, were goaded by divine grace, and taking up the rule of the monastic order, they asked to be clothed with the holy veil. Carrying out the duties and offices of a good shepherd to them, Blessed Winefride sometimes taught them to be fortified against the ambushes of the deceitful devil by the words of the gospels and the sayings of the holy fathers, and sometimes by the splendid expression of her own discourse she poured divine love into their hearts. Moreover, she did not cease to instruct them with constant admonitions, to direct them wisely toward the precepts of the rule, to be mindful of her way of life and to be dutiful in these things. In truth, she did without ceasing the same things which she taught should be done by those subject to her. Certainly every day she zealously directed them toward fasts and prayers and vigils, and by doing these things herself she showed how the virgins subject to her ought to live; the model of the flock entrusted to her became an example of living rightly. Moreover, reaching in a short time the pinnacle of all virtues, she made it known openly that Christ, the Virtue of God and the Wisdom of God, possessed the fullness of her heart. And indeed, on the one hand, countless powers and frequent miracles clearly manifested this, and on the other hand, doctrines of salvation flowing abundantly from her mouth demonstrated that plainly. Furthermore, the convent of virgins increased exceedingly, with the fragrance of that good order drawing them to the knowledge of God and pouring the love of the Deity into their hearts. That holy community used to rejoice that such a woman presided over it, one in whom it visibly beheld that all exercises of virtue overflowed, and it recognised that heavenly grace shone copiously in her. Therefore, since she applied herself assiduously to all her practices of the heavenly life, the neighbours all around began to be devout through love of her; moreover, those situated far away were much pleased on account of her good reputation, saying that those to whom she was nearer, either by her way of life or her acquaintance, were steeped in the very great mercy of God. And many displays of powers happened through her in miracles. That fact clearly subjected even more the hearts of fierce men to her devotion, and also compelled the minds of the faithful to show reverence to her, and winning over the favour of all equally, drew it to her. Now it was quite agreeable to everyone to remain in the vicinity, with certain ones very much striving after the delight of the total good and the way of salvation through her, and certain ones truly believing the power of heavenly grace to be in her on account of the favours brought to them outwardly in miracles. And so with all accepting with great veneration and reverence the divine splendour which shone through her far and wide in that district, the virgins subject to her, those to whom it showed itself more brightly, advanced more after that. In fact, seeing her sigh to God with groans each day, and seeing divine utterances come frequently to her, they took up a greater devotion to God and were made ever better.

19

Truly, when Blessed Winefride was pursuing good works of this kind with perseverance, and through her the heavenly light was shining all around, very often calling to mind the memory of her master's words and precepts, she thought that the day of his departure was drawing near, namely, the day on which he had departed from her and commanded that a gift be sent to him. Moreover, keeping this in her memory with unceasing earnestness, by her own toil and that of her virgins, she made a chasuble of one single texture to be despatched to the man of God. And so, the day dawning on which that present was to be sent, which is the first of May, the blessed maiden came with many others to the spring in which she was to place her gift according to the command of the man of God. First she took up the chasuble and wrapped it in a white cloth and thus placed it in the middle of the spring, saying that she was directing it to the blessed man, Beuno, through the agency of the spring. And behold - a thing wondrous to say and unbelievable except to a man of faith - that small piece of cloth in which the chasuble was wrapped suffered no injury from the water nor did it experience even the least infusion of water, but remaining altogether dry with the chasuble, it was carried by the rush of the flowing water and conveyed on the great stream. And that whole day and the following night, that gift of the maiden was carried over the waves of the sea; in the morning it was cast upon that shore on which the holy man had built his dwellings. Moreover, when Blessed Beuno went out from the church in the morning, he stood upon the edge of the sea, and he was regarding with admiration how the waters that had first rushed forth then returned to themselves, and with what hidden force they drew the waves to themselves; by chance he spied at a distance on the shore the wrapped cloth. Going nearer, he tried to know with more certainty what that was, and, after he had put his hand to it, lifting it from the sand of the sea and unfolding the wrapped cloth, he found the chasuble, which had no damage to it at all. The cloth, also, which had covered it on the outside appeared dry, just as if it had not touched the water. And indeed, while he was thinking carefully and trying to discern the reason for this discovery, and at the same time wondering at the fact that he could find something not drenched within the watery strands of soaked sand, the memory of Winefride, the maiden beloved of God, came secretly into his mind. When he had reflected on how he had ordered her to prepare a gift for him every year and to place what was prepared in the spring which flowed into the river, at last he recognised, with the Holy Spirit revealing it to him, that it had been sent by the blessed maiden, conveyed unharmed to him from the blessed maiden over the gulf of the sea. Then humbly giving thanks to God, he freely accepted that gift and placed it in the church to be kept thereafter for his use as well as that of the other servants of God. And he rejoiced exceedingly because the blessed maiden had been mindful of his words, and because her reputation was so excellent that by it nearly the whole district had been illuminated. Moreover, he prayed to the Lord that an increase of virtues be magnified in her, and that whatever was pleasing in His eyes be found in manifold ways in her, and that the consciences of others be inflamed with heavenly devotion through her.

20

Truly, it is clear enough from the outcome that God accepted his prayers and showed to him the hearkening ears of His mercy. For indeed, the practice of the heavenly way of life had advanced in the maiden to such a great extent that the sum of all perfection was found in her, and, like a solitary splendour, she appeared to the people of the whole district, both present and absent, as a model of living and an example of doing good. Also, she had a wondrous, divine power to persuade what she wished, for as often as she received a talent of the divine word entrusted to her to be dispensed to others, so great an ability in speech came to her and so temperate a seriousness in her judgments that her words generally touched all and bound them in devotion to God. Thereafter, nearly all the inhabitants of that country, restrained by her repeated admonitions, abstained from all the things which could hinder their salvation, and with burning eagerness they directed themselves to the things which they knew to be works of faith and which they saw the blessed maiden or her fellow nuns strive after. Truly, she showed herself to be devoted to everything which Beuno, the blessed man, had said or commanded, certainly neglecting nothing of all which had been enjoined upon her. Indeed, every year on the first of May she sent a gift to her master, while he was alive, in the manner in which we indicated above; and although a great space separated them from each other (for fifty miles or more made up the distance between them), yet in the space of one night, carried over the winding currents of the sea to the door of the monastery, the gift was found in the morning on the sand of the shore. Moreover, for this reason a name was bestowed on the blessed man which is kept as a remembrance even today among the people of Wales, for he is called Beuno Casul Sech, that is, Beuno Dry Chasuble, because the dry chasuble was conveyed to him over the waters, unharmed by the waters. Furthermore, while the maiden observed this manner of sending the gift every year, it happened that blessed Beuno, worn out by old age, went to his heavenly joy, full of virtues and renowned for good works, leaving behind this frail world filled with hardships. Records indicating the manner of his life and his ways, records concerning his life or his passing, and what he did as a youth, or what miracles he performed after death, are still kept in respectful memory. This outstanding memorial is also proclaimed about him, that after death he performed many more miracles than while living.

21

When his death became known to the holy maiden, she honoured him with many tears and prayers, and she ceased to send the afore-mentioned gift any longer. Moreover, then for the first time saying that she was destitute of all human consolation, she began to be weary of the place in which she lived, and with time passing little by little, when most of her fellow-nuns had departed from this world, she began to hate the place in which she had dwelt thus far. Mindful of her teacher's words, by which he had indicated that after seven years she ought to look for another place and live there, at the completion of the final year she began to dislike the place and to neglect completely all the various buildings. And since her face was that of a person turning her attention elsewhere, her spirit had no rest while she stayed there. Yet, not until the aforementioned seven years were finished did she have the ability to abandon that dwelling or to go elsewhere. But indeed, when all the years had passed, then having taken control over herself and lifting her mind with every effort toward God, she prayed that He would direct her to a place where she could please herself and profit others; and that He would deign to pour forth His blessings upon that place in which she had first received consolation, so that one who might come there for the sake of prayer or of finding some cure would gain what he asked for when her name had been invoked, with those pleading on his behalf who for love of her had corrected their own actions and habits. Countless peoples released from the infirmities of different diseases in that place bear witness that this request reached the ears of God. Hereafter this will be shown by clear examples, when first we have composed the narrative of this history.

22

Therefore, when the blessed maiden, Winefride, gave herself earnestly to prayer, begging that God's mercy would sustain her and be the guide of her journey, as she was intent upon vigils and prayers on a certain night, a divine utterance of this kind came to her: "With only one maiden with you as your companion, go to Blessed Deifer, who dwells in the place called Botavarrus, and when he has been consulted, you will know what then you are to do or where you are to go." Indeed, that man was great in the sight of God, one who walked in all commandments and ordinances without complaint. Of him it is recorded that, since he abounded plentifully in the grace of miraculous powers, he caused a spring to burst forth from the earth, and that after it had been blessed by his outstretched hand, he had prayed to God that any sick person who immersed himself in it would return to his own home in possession of his health. Many people who obtained their health there have asserted that this was done. Indeed, although very many miracles accomplished by him are recorded in numerous reports, yet it is pleasing to introduce in particular one performed after his death, since, when that has been considered carefully, it is readily known whose merit it was. Certain thieves going out to commit robbery found two horses in the cemetery of Blessed Deifer; leading them off, they hoped to get away without hindrance. However, the masters of those horses, coming to the cemetery in which they had left them and not finding them there, knew that they had been stolen. They returned to their lodgings, made candles, and, entering the church of the most holy confessor, placed them upon the altar. Since these were not lighted, nor did they have at hand fire with which to light them, they humbly prayed to the saint of God that either he light them with a light sent from Heaven, or that he accept them unlighted with the same zeal as if they were given to him lighted. Indeed, showing that he was attentive to their prayers, the saint lighted their candles with a sudden light when they had been placed before him. For this reason a greater devotion to Saint Deifer increased in them, and the hope of recovering what they had wrongfully lost arose in them. Nor was their expectation deceived, for the aforementioned thieves, after wandering over the entire surrounding district, when about midnight they thought that they had fled far away, eagerly wanting to know where they had come, finally realised that they had arrived at the hedge by which the aforementioned cemetery was encircled. Moved by mighty anguish and knowing that, if caught, they would not have committed that robbery with impunity, they tried again with reins loosed to flee. But neither was divine power weak then to show the hand of its strength against them, for when they thought that they were far removed, since the light of day had burst forth, they had been led back to the aforementioned place and were forced to dismount from the horses and hold the reins in their hands within the perimeter of the same cemetery. Moreover, the men who had lost the horses had not yet departed from the same place, but, having waited in the church for a while, they believed that some solace would come to them soon through the Lord's saint. Therefore, coming out of the church as day was dawning, they saw that their own horses stood in the churchyard, and the same men who had led them there were holding them. Then, praising God and giving thanks to Saint Deifer, they took their horses, allowing the thieves to depart unpunished. So, from these summaries one can easily infer how much merit was in the holy man to whom Blessed Winefride was commanded to go by the divine utterance.

23

And so, the most holy maiden, entrusting to God her abode and all with whom she had dwelt, began her travels, content with only one maiden as her companion, as she had heard in the divine utterance. Coming to Saint Deifer (it is well known that he was at a distance of about eight miles from the place where she had started out), she was received by him with great kindness. When they had watched in prayer for a long time, they sat together while the maiden explained completely the reason for her coming to him. The holy man responded to her in this way: "I am as yet truly unaware of this divine counsel," he said, "but be patient a while and pass the night here with us. Perhaps the Lord will deign to reveal something to us which might be pleasing to Himself and a summary of your plan." She willingly assented to this, knowing without a doubt that it had been made known to her from the heavenly response given to her that she would be taught by this same saint what they were to do. Thus, to the saint who was praying throughout that entire night (as he was accustomed to do), a voice came from Heaven saying: "Tell my dearest daughter, the maiden Winefride, to go to the village called Henthlant; there she will obtain in some measure what she earnestly desires, for she will find there a venerable man named Saturnus. Through him she will hear in full what she will do next, for instance, in what place she will dwell for the rest of her life." And so, summoning the maiden to himself in the morning, Saint Deifer kept back nothing of all which he had been divinely taught. Showing her the way by which she ought to proceed to the aforementioned saint, he advised her to go joyfully, telling her that it had been made known to him from Heaven that she would hear openly from that saint what was right for her, and the entire order of what she should do.

24

Indeed, Blessed Winefride rejoiced because, with every doubt removed, she had been led by Blessed Deifer to some certainty, and because she knew that God was taking care of her. Saying farewell to the most holy man, she and her companion undertook their journey to Blessed Saturnus. When she came to him, she was received most kindly by him. In fact, made aware of her whole plan and journey beforehand by a response given to him on this matter from on high, he received the blessed maiden with every sentiment of devotion. Then, he advised that she remain with him that night and on the next day she would be fully instructed concerning all that she required; she agreed and, led first to prayer, she sat down with him, saying that she had come to him at God's command so that by his teaching she might obtain her desire. And so, remaining there that whole night, in the morning she heard from Blessed Saturnus words of this kind: "There is a certain place called Witheriac, a place filled with the relics of many saints; it was chosen by God on account of their venerable manner of living, and it is held in very great awe by all the people. God commands you to visit this place, and while you are alive to dwell there in person and to instruct the souls of others by your example. A certain abbot named Elerius is there, a man of many virtues. Continual lamentation and persistent prayer have so rendered him free and purified of all secular cares that, now intent entirely on things of Heaven, he savours nothing earthly; he aspires to nothing at all of worldly pleasure. I have been admonished by a divine command to send you to him, and, moreover, to tell you that there you will find whatever is necessary in the present life to satisfy a soul longing for the things of Heaven. For in that place are virgins consecrated to God, from the very beginnings of their childhood observing celibacy in the profession of the religious life and exerting themselves in their purpose with diligent devotion; to a certain degree they must be made better, God willing, by your instruction and example. For although they keep themselves in the service of Christ by ever-watchful observance, yet by your coming they will be made more devout, and a greater splendour of divinity will shine upon them."

25

When she had heard about the virgins' manner of living, Winefride, alluding much to their praise, confessed that she was long since bound by the same ardent desire, and that she wished most gladly to embrace the name of virginity with them; moreover, she asked that a guide for the way be provided for her as quickly as possible. Indeed, assigning his own deacon to the blessed maiden and through him sending her to Blessed Elerius, Saint Saturnus began himself to lead her a little way. And when he had told her many things about the loveliness of the place to which she was going while they were speaking, at last, wishing to depart from her, he imparted the blessing requested of him. Then, asking that many good things be granted to her by God, the saint returned to his own home, and she made her way to where she was going. Knowing of her arrival beforehand through the Holy Spirit, the saintly man quickly set out to meet her, and he received that most faithful worshipper of God as was fitting; the deacon who had come with her told everything which had been divinely intimated to his teacher, and how she had been sent to that place by the admonition of God. When she had first been properly greeted and honoured with due respect, he led her into the church to pray; when the prayer was finished, the saint embraced the maiden and exhorted her to be of steadfast spirit. Calling her afterwards to a private meeting, he inquired about what she conceived in her mind and what she had resolved to do: "For," he said, "although the whole manner of your life has been made known to my humble self from on high - how you were initiated into the divine mysteries; in what way you obtained the glory of martyrdom by the severing of your head; what are the marks of your suffering and your blood poured out - yet, I wish to be taught from your own mouth the reason which compels you to take up the hardship of so great a journey." The maiden responded to him thus: "The One who deigned to reveal to you what you have just now made known has not left you entirely unknowing, I think, concerning the things which I am turning over in my mind, or why I have come to this place. For as it was possible for you to reveal what had happened to me in the past, so it was equally possible to show plainly what will befall me in the future. Therefore, receive me, sent to you by God, and so arrange my way of life now as was shown to you before by heavenly utterance." Then the holy man decided to defer the explanation of this plan for that night which was near at hand, and he humbly entreated her to bear it patiently.

26

And so while Saint Elerius devoted himself to prayer through the whole night, and Blessed Winefride likewise was intent with ever-watchful constancy upon her prayers, certainty in this matter was made evident to the holy confessor as he rested a little around daybreak. Made very glad by this, he came to the maiden in the morning, and, rushing to her embrace, he advised her to rejoice and to be free from care thereafter. Then, indeed, taking her hand, he led her into the convent of virgins which, as we have said before, was renowned in that place; he addressed them with these words: "Dearest Daughters, be very attentive with your minds, for it is important to make known to you with how great a splendour the Divine Mercy has deigned to shine upon you with compassion. Behold, It has determined to send this maiden consecrated to It to remain with you and to dwell with you, so that by observing her life you will be made more devoted in God's service by her example, and a reward will be given to her in Heaven because of your improvement. This is that maiden, Winefride, whose great fame flew to your ears some time ago: in order not to suffer the loss of her chastity, she scorned the attacks of her pursuers together with the enticements of flatterers, and to the last she chose to die willingly by decapitation for the safeguarding of her virginity. This is the one, I say, whose signs of triumph shine far and wide through the Church; because of her titles of honour that whole district boasts that it is granted a great good. She alone is not unaware that she will receive from God the palm of martyrdom and of outstanding accomplishment. Therefore, to you she has come, to remain with you and to await the day of her death, she who has already claimed Heaven by her merits, and whose place of retribution among the blessed martyrs is secured. And so, be exceedingly glad at her coming and devoutly embrace the heavenly treasure dwelling among you, carefully paying attention to her works and imitating her with every effort. Indeed, the Most High has sent her here to this place so that you, while observing her, might store up your merits with hers in Heaven, and so that this place might be sprinkled with much fame on account of her while this world endures." After these words, he turned to one woman (who was his own mother and the superior for the other nuns) and said: "To you, O Dearest Mother, I especially entrust the care of this maiden dear to God. Thus, you follow in her footsteps, you imitate her works, you pursue with earnest skill the care of all things which pertain to her or whatever you know pleases Him. Let it be known to you and to the others sitting in our presence that this blessed maiden has been sent to this place by divine utterance; for this reason, you ought to have greater devotion around her, and you ought not to be unaware of how great a care this place is in the sight of God." When these words had been spoken, the confessor departed, and Blessed Winefride remained to pass her life from then on with the handmaidens of God.

27

And then, indeed, she hastened to seize the summit of all religious life, and she stood steadfastly on the peak of all virtues, as if thus far she had been utterly a stranger to this kind of sanctity. And since the first prophetic signs of her manner of life had been revealed to the holy virgins by the blessed man, she entered upon every path of salvation with such burning devotion, as if then for the first time she had begun to be converted to God. In her there was continual abstinence and guarding of her goodness, and persevering prayer for holiness, and humble living. In her the other virgins received an example of patience and obedience, and they made her a leader for themselves in all things which pertained to salvation. In her they found copiously all things which were of integrity and virtue. Thus, they showed her great respect. In fact, the one who was their superior (Theonia was her name), that is to say, the mother of Elerius, the holy confessor, loved her with earnest affection, and with Winefride's advice she managed the care of herself as well as the other maidens entrusted to her. Indeed, she reverenced the watchful constancy in her, and she marveled at her continuous abstinence, and she cherished in her the perseverance with sweet joy in all virtues. Very often, also, while discussing with her their longings for the heavenly kingdom, she caused tears to flow copiously from Winefride's eyes, and she wept as well, for she was truly a woman of great dignity and extraordinary holiness, and one zealously attentive to all works of charity and mercy. Although she loved all the maidens with inestimable devotion, yet she received Saint Winefride with joyful affection, and she paid much attention to her venerableness. To be sure, Saint Elerius, who served the Lord separately with his brothers and fellow-disciples in simplicity of heart and with great affliction of spirit, sometimes came to her and set her before the others to be imitated. Moreover, very often while talking with her about the hidden things of Heaven, sometimes even about the mysteries of the Church, he found her to be overflowing abundantly concerning things which pertain to God, and to be rich in intelligent understanding of the outward necessities of life. Thus he would return to his own brothers, admiring in her both the profusion of outward knowledge and the fullness of divine grace within. And he could not long conceal this from the people nearby, from which that place in a short time gained great renown and was held in great respect. In fact, faithful people from everywhere used to hasten there in crowds wishing to see the maiden formerly decapitated for love of Christ, but brought to life again by the charitable deed of a certain saint, crowds gloriously proclaiming that the place in which she dwelt was worthy of the highest reverence. In truth, to certain ones the sight of her alone was enough, and speaking to her; however, some who acted more importunately asked humbly that the place of the cutting on the maiden's neck be shown to them. She feared to resist their requests, lest their devotion be lessened on that account, and lest that be imputed to pride in her. Those who saw on her neck the skin covering over the place of the cutting growing white with a wondrous colour could not refrain from tears. Blessing God in His mighty works and filled with very great wonder, they returned to their own places.

28

In fact, on a certain day Blessed Elerius entered the nuns' cloister to visit the holy maiden, Winefride, and to discuss with her the things of the Lord. Moreover, while they were speaking to each other at length, by chance the conversation came to the memory of death. Then, since an occasion was found for bringing forth what he very often reflected on in his mind, the saint said: "I rejoice that God has sent you to this place to consign my body to its burial and to keep the memory of me after my death. For I have often prayed that this be granted to me by God, namely, that someone might send here one of his servants or handmaidens who would bury me and, dwelling in this place after me, would make it famous." To him the blessed maiden replied thus: "Indeed, it will not be so, nor so has it been preordained by God. For it is necessary that you first commit to the earth your mother, my superior, while I survive and stay with you, and at last, after the course of some years, to bury my body. Then, full of days, you will finish your life in peace and, conveyed to your fathers, you will find in the heavenly kingdom what you have stored there to be preserved." When he had heard these words, the holy confessor departed. Moreover, it was soon apparent that she had spoken a true prophecy, for after a short span of time Blessed Theonia was seized by a serious illness, and she began to be beset by the stings of death now coming upon her. When her daughters, that is to say the virgins who were under her discipline, recognised her swift departure, they began to languish with much weeping and sorrow. Indeed, they were lamenting exceedingly because they were losing a mother who had nourished them and reared them in the service of God and taught them the divine mysteries. Comforting them with expressions of solace, she used to say that mournful words ought to be uttered at the time when worse succeeds better and when divine laws perish through evil successors; truly, when better succeeds good and the things which are God's are carried to an ever-better state, then grief and desolation should not be allowed, but rather it is the duty of a man who possesses a good habit of mind to accept with a glad heart, with spiritual joy, the improvement sent from on high. "And you," she said, "ought therefore to bear my death patiently, since you will have with you this blessed maiden, Winefride, in whom you can sufficiently find all that pertains to doctrine or to a model of salvation. Observe her with your inner eyes and imitate her with the desire of your soul. Direct your steps to her as if to a singular star, and devote the care of all your deeds to her, knowing without a doubt that God is your helper in all things if you give willing assent to the counsels of that maiden." After these words, she received the life-giving communion of the Lord's body and blood from her son, namely the holy confessor, Elerius, and departing instantly from this world, she gave up her spirit into the hands of the holy angels.

29

After she had been properly laid to rest, as was fitting for so great a woman, and buried with the great lamentation and weeping of all, the holy man entrusted the custody and care of the other virgins to Blessed Winefride. Although she strove much to resist his command, yet fearing God's judgment if she tried to withstand longer, finally she consented and added the care of the others to her own burden. Now, indeed, it is not possible to report with how great a determination of total abstinence she took these austerities upon herself, what torments or how great the penalties she imposed on her own body, of how much sparingness or strictness were in her. In truth, (so that I might explain everything fully), she left absolutely nothing untried which she knew pertained to her own salvation or lead to an example and advantage for others. Thus, established in these ways, she was loved with sincere affection by all; both strangers and members of her own household showed honour to her and respectfully did homage to her. In fact, Blessed Elerius and other very great men who lived in Wales, seeing such great perfection in the maiden, deferred much to her and revered her. All the powerful men and nobles of the country embraced her with sweet devotion and, seeing her kind way of life, they were very much edified. Also, many men of lesser rank, coming to her and observing the modesty of her appearance, and receiving great edification from her sermons, thereafter were made more disposed to the service of God. But even robbers and usurpers of others' property were remorseful at heart after they had seen the appearance of her countenance and heard her sermons. And certain of these were then made milder; indeed, some, ceasing their robberies altogether, were converted to the Lord, doing public penance for their crimes. And (that I might include everything precisely), no age, no sex, likewise no man of any business within that country seemed left who did not have some benefit from the good deeds of this maiden. Then Saint Elerius, the friend of God, was unutterably glad, and sometimes he preached to the people about her, saying, among other things, that God had sent her to that same country for the enlightening of the faithful people, and that the power of the Divinity dwelt in her. Many people knew this clearly enough, for countless miracles and cures of the sick granted through her bore powerful witness that she had the power of divinity. Indeed, whoever came to her sick left in good condition after his health had been recovered. The one who came sad went away rejoicing; one who came oppressed at heart by any trouble or burdened by some outward cause befalling him returned to his own place cheerful, immediately freed from the cares weighing him down, and having gained his wish. Certainly, she harmed no one, but in some way benefitted all commonly and individuals particularly. Indeed, whoever dwelt in the area of that estate and was beset by misfortunes of body or soul quickly obtained his desired remedy through her. She kept herself so apart from all worldly entanglements that she considered herself impure if she allowed for her own use or among the necessities of her associates even the smallest of all the things which belong to the pomp of this world. She also exercised temperance in her admiration of all things. She remained zealous in the care of the virgins subject to her; she made them cautious and sufficiently learned to avoid even the subtleties of the cunning Foe. Truly, in her sermons and constant prayers she defended them from the enemy of the human race and the attacker of the Lord's law by tirelessly warning that they be circumspect in all their actions, and that they have a constant concern for their own salvation.

30

Thus, during this time, after Winefride, the maiden beloved of God, had led a life acceptable to the King on high in its devoted service, it happened that, behold, the Lord Jesus, wishing to take up His handmaid from the toilsome service of this life to the rest of everlasting happiness, indicated to her on a certain night as she was devoting herself to prayers in the chapel that the day of her death was very near. As soon as she sensed that she had been called, she knew immediately that she had been visited by the grace of God, and with an exultant spirit she began to prepare herself for the joys of the everlasting kingdom. Then on successive nights she used to spend the night praying in church, and in the days she persisted with total effort in every virtue, leaving nothing undone, according to her strength, of all which she had learned should be done. Moreover, to the virgins staying with her she announced that her departure was to occur soon. When they heard this, the handmaids of God began to be moved by sorrow and tormented by inconsolable grief. Trying to comfort them with consolations, the blessed maiden used to say that they ought not to be sad on account of bodily separation, since she was passing from corruption to incorruption, from miseries to joys; they ought rather to be very glad and to rejoice with her because she was going to such a Lord, with Whom she could intercede for them and protect them as much as possible. She even exhorted them to beware of the cunning of the Enemy who steals deceitfully, teaching them that there are many-shaped subtleties in his slyness; she exhorted them especially to depend on her examples and to show themselves such that they might deserve to be aided by her intercessions. Moreover, as soon as that rumour was brought to the attention of Blessed Elerius, he was particularly distressed by exceedingly great sorrows over the departure of the maiden dear to him. In fact, knowing that she had been divinely given a gift of special grace, he wished with very great piety that she remain with him while he sojourned in the body. Now, moreover, although she was passing from misfortune and hardships to joy lasting without end, with himself left behind amidst the disorders of the world, he used to say with regret that he was losing the solace of his earthly sojourn. Yet, bringing himself often into her presence and engaging in conversations, as if in offering himself to her, he carried out the duties and habits of a good shepherd, by having concern for her in all things and by carefully supplying what he knew would be beneficial to her.

31

Meanwhile, the blessed maiden began to be troubled by serious internal pain. When her illness was strong and increasing daily, she knew that she was bound by the incitements of her death. Then, turning her attention to God with her whole strength, she prayed that He have mercy on her, and that He be the faithful overseer and guardian of her soul so that she would not become the plunder of the most wicked Plunderer. Then, when Elerius, the holy confessor, had been called to her, she fortified herself with the last sacrament of the Lord's body and blood. In truth, seeing the virgins, her companions, afflicted with very great sorrow on account of her sickness, she encouraged them with words of comfort, saying, "Do not, Daughters, do not be troubled with excessive sadness on account of my death, since by the mercy of God I shall come to the highest immutable good when the present misery has been left behind. Now I rejoice that I rejected an earthly spouse, that inflamed by love of God alone I trampled upon all the world's pleasures, or that I decided to have nothing of my own in this world. And so, be assured that now I shall come to Him Whom I have preferred to all things, and in comparison to Whom I have judged all worldly goods to be as dung. Know, I say, that I shall enjoy the sight of Him forever, for love of Whom I made myself a detriment, and I despised all the delights of the flesh. Therefore, with loving devotion embrace so good and great a Lord, with your entire effort rely on the examples of salvation proposed to you and made clear to you, and strive to keep your covenant with the heavenly spouse to Whom you promised to guard your faith and your chastity. For with His help alone you can await this day with sure hope; you can avoid the ambushes of your enemies and have everlasting peace. In fact, consider trivial and momentary whatever presents itself to your eyes of flesh. Indeed, you ought not pay attention to things which are here today and vanish tomorrow, nor to turn your soul away from those immutable goods which never fail, in which there are peace and freedom from care and everlasting joy." After these words she turned to prayer and asked earnestly that her soul be taken up by the hands of the Lord.

32

And so, on the first day of November she began to be severely weakened by the dissolution of her body. But even then amidst her pains she did not rest from salutary preaching, for she instructed all who came to her by advising them to watch carefully the end of her life, showing how much happiness they would have who left this life with souls cleansed and purified of the world's filth. When her body was made feeble by the exceeding gravity of her illness, and she perceived that her death was now near at hand, she asked Blessed Elerius, who had been called to her, that her body be given up for burial next to the body of his mother, Blessed Theonia. When the holy man most kindly granted this, turning again to prayer, on that same day, that is November 2, she commended her spirit into the hands of the Creator to be joined to the heavenly choir. Seeing this, those who were there gave way to most vehement lamentations on account of her departure. What groaning, what outpouring of tears was there then? No one was free from wailing; each sex and age turned itself to profuse lamentation, and the more each one believed that she counseled and aided him, so much the greater sorrow did he feel on account of her absence. Although the mourning was unbearable for all, an enormous grief affected especially the virgins who had lived with her; indeed, they were lamenting aloud that they had lost their mistress and their teacher of salvation.

33

And so, with all lamenting her departure in a different way, Blessed Elerius, hastening to them with words of consolation, imposed silence on them. Then, commending her soul to God, he began with care to attend to everything that seemed to pertain to the blessed maiden's final rites. Thereafter, he ordered the body, prepared in the manner of those to be buried, to be carried into the church. When everything that pertained to the funeral or burial had been completed, the body was consigned to the earth, accompanied by the very great lamentation of all, in that place which she had requested. Indeed, many men of great merit also rest in the same cemetery; even the famous and most holy confessors, Chebius and Senanus, are reported to be there. The first of these is buried at her head; indeed, the other rests in the same row in which she lies. Certainly they are remembered among the native people there to have been men of great virtues, and to have come to the same place on account of the multitude of saints whom they heard had gathered there to complete the struggle of the present life. In the same district there still exist some churches in their memory, in which their great merit before God is shown clearly to men through numerous miracles. Buried to the left of Winefride rests Blessed Theonia, about whom we reported above; God alone knows the names and number of the other saints who repose there. Indeed, that place is held to be venerable due to so great a gathering of saints that no mortal at all could know their names or even comprehend the number of those gathered. With all of these the blessed maiden, Winefride, famous for virtues and illustrious for her countless miracles, adorns the same place. Truly, after her death, many who came there and sought from God a cure for their infirmities through her aid obtained the desired remedies. Moreover, that place was held in great renown and was sought out with great reverence and veneration by many for the sake of prayer. In fact, after a period of some years, Blessed Elerius, a man of highest sanctity and exceeding perfection, departed to the Lord, leaving this life filled with every holiness and piety. Buried in the church of his own name, he has not ceased to be illustrious for his many miracles even to this day; bringing much respect and dignity to this place, he is renowned for his very many miracles.

34

Truly, the place in which the first signs of the blessed maiden's way of life were evident is considered venerable, with much visitation of the faithful. For often very clear miracles happen there under the gaze of the blessed maiden, through which those coming know that Blessed Winefride can succour their injuries, and because of that a throng of faithful people devoutly rush there in troops from all sides, hoping that they will obtain cures for their bodies and souls through her prayers. Moreover, the devotion of those coming there is increased daily, of those seeing the very swift spring which burst from the place where the virgin's head first fell to the earth, and of those looking at the stones which lie in the bottom of the stream; with her blood still preserved on these, it is evident that they grew red through the martyrdom of the maiden. When many flock around with minds disposed to see this, observing that the blood adhering to the stones cannot be washed away by the constant flowing of water running over them, they marvel at the strangeness of the thing, and they return to their own places glorifying the special privilege of the maiden. Many infirm persons also come there and, made well, return to their own homes.

35

A certain workman living in that country had a daughter blind from birth. Hearing that many people had been granted their health through the merits of Blessed Winefride, with very great devotion he took his daughter (who was asking every day to be taken) to the spring of the holy maiden. Brought there at a late hour, she first bathed her head in the spring, and then she was taken to the church to pray there without sleeping for the whole night. While this was happening, at dawn she asked that she be permitted to sleep a little. When this had been granted to her and a place prepared for her to rest, she slept for a long time; then awaking, she declared that she saw well. Moreover, observing her and learning that it was just as she was asserting, her father made known what God had effected with respect to his daughter on account of the merits of Saint Winefride, and with his words stirring all who were present to proclaim the praises of the maiden, he returned with his daughter to his own home. Because of this miracle many people, inflamed in their devotion to the blessed maiden, were proclaiming here and there to all listening the mighty works of her miraculous powers. In truth, through wondrous works of this kind which happened on account of her, certain ones, clinging to her with ardent love, went to her as if to a singular refuge, and after a little while, having obtained their wishes, they returned to their homes. This will be shown clearly from the example below.

36

By chance a considerable disturbance occurred at a certain time in those parts. When the more noble and powerful men of that province had sent a messenger to their friends in the vicinity so that they might set a careful watch on their property and be very cautiously on guard for themselves, their courier, surrounded by robbers, swiftly took flight to the church of the blessed maiden, Winefride. Moreover, with his enemies ever-following him by his tracks, he entered the churchyard on the horse he was riding, leapt down from the horse at the door of the church, and secured the bridle by tying it to the bar of the door. Then, also wanting to avoid the enemies who were drawing very near to him, he ran swiftly to the altar. However, one of the robbers, bolder than the others, a man who did not respect God nor His saints, entering the enclosure with bold presumption, came on the run to the horse; seizing the bridle with outstretched hand and loosing it from the bar of the gate, he led the horse away without any fear at all of the maiden's punishment. Indeed, the man to whom the horse belonged came out of the church and did not find the horse where he had left it. Moreover, knowing that his horse had been taken by those who had followed him as he fled, he again entered the church; there putting his complaint before God and the blessed maiden, he lamented bitterly the violence brought against him and that he could not find peace within the enclosure of the church. Earnestly asking the maiden, Saint Winefride, with great supplication that she be mindful of that presumptuous and overly-bold arrogance, and that she bring swift vengeance for the crime committed, while going out of the church he was compelled to follow on foot the way upon which the rider had started. After a short time, truly, the blessed maiden showed that the violation of her churchyard and her church was a concern to her, and she made clear that she does not ever heedlessly neglect a complaint brought to her with lamentation. Indeed, the man who had loosed the horse tied to the church door and led him away began to grow weak due to a very serious sickness. Also, after a little while that weakness was drawn from the whole body and conveyed itself entirely to his right arm; it took hold upon the wretched man, bringing him such great misery and affliction that he preferred to die rather than to be afflicted by such great distress. The torment even grew by daily increases, and it could not be relieved by any physician's cure. It did not cease until that entire arm with its hand, putrefied from the noxious fluid that had gathered there, fell from the rest of the body after excessive, unbearable sufferings. But not even then could that most wretched man rest or entirely escape his former troubles until, coming to the aforementioned church of the blessed maiden, he humbly acknowledged her merits and begged forgiveness for the crime he had committed. Then, indeed, relieved somewhat from his violent pain through the mercy of the holy maiden, he was kept there as a warning to others. Fortunately, at the sight of him all who lay in ambush for the property of others were terrified, and they were warned in a dreadful way that none should intrude beyond the churchyard. In addition, all who saw that that man had been punished for such boldness and wretched audacity by so lamentable a recompense marveled at the maiden's merits and became more devout in her service. In fact, the one who had lost his arm, while making satisfaction to the blessed maiden by public penance because he had burst into the enclosure of her church with rash boldness and had raised his hand against her, restrained many from presumption of this kind. People rushed in throngs from all quarters wishing to see that unusual miracle, and when it had been seen, they returned full of wonder, grandly proclaiming the maiden's praises.

37

Also, another no less wondrous miracle was brought to pass through Blessed Winefride. In a certain district of the aforementioned church, thieves who showed no respect for the blessed maiden led away with them by stealth a cow which they found. However, fearing that the people who lived nearby might follow them and be guided to them directly by the tracks of the cow they were leading away, they turned to a hard, stony path on which they thought that neither their tracks nor the animal's tracks could be seen. In truth, there is no counsel;

there is no wisdom nor strength against the Lord! Indeed, as they proceeded on the rocky way on which they thought to hide themselves more completely, their wickedness first began to be detected there. For immediately the cow drove its hooves into the ground as far as the knees, and the animal's tracks were clearly evident on the stones just as on the hard, dry path. The more they thought they were proceeding secretly, the more there was recognition of their flight, with God manifesting the merits of the maiden through their steps. In fact, the farther they proceeded, the safer they believed it would be for them, and the more securely they trusted that they would keep what they had taken. But it turned out to the contrary for them. For when those from whom the cow had been stolen learned that their animal had been taken from them by stealth, they began immediately to pursue the thieves with a very great troop of men. Observing the animal's tracks impressed on the stones and the dry earth, they were made more certain and carefully followed the impression of the hooves. Invoking the aid of the blessed maiden through whose merits they saw so evident a miracle in the rocks and in the hard ground, they rushed along the way indicated to them by the cow's tracks. In fact, hearing the shouts of those pursuing them and fearing that they would be caught by them with the animal which they were leading, the robbers departed from the path. But they could not be concealed in this way, for those following wherever they went always found the impressions of the animal's hooves clearly in the rocks and in the dry soil; strengthened in spirit and comforted by the miracle shown to them, they pursued with confidence. And the thieves, recognising that the farther they proceeded, so ever-clearer were the animal's tracks, and that they could by no means escape unless they sought flight in different directions after the cow was released, they left it in a grove and, fleeing very swiftly, they hid themselves. In fact, those who were pursuing them, finding the cow alone after those who were leading it away had fled, took what was theirs and began to go back. Moreover, examining carefully whether their animal made tracks of this kind in the stones and the earth while going back, as it had made when it was led away, they found none at all. Then indeed they knew that the blessed maiden had worked that miracle for their sakes, namely, so that through the animal's tracks they might recognise where they ought to proceed, and they might pursue more rapidly what had been taken from them by unjust pillage. In fact, upon returning they restored the cow to its own master and publicly proclaimed the miracle that had been performed. Also, many people went out to see what was said about the tracks, and finding what was proclaimed to be true, they themselves did not cease to proclaim the same things as well. On account of this all who gaped with longing at the possessions of others and plotted deception in their heart were exceedingly terrified, and they were especially warned in an amazing way that they should not snatch away anything or in any way commit robbery within the district that extended to the church of the blessed maiden. Moreover, fearing the maiden's anger and fearing that God, grievously displeased because of the contempt for her, might avenge their presumptuous boldness, and that they would thus suffer punishment, the robbers came to the church of the holy maiden begging forgiveness with humble hearts. Confessing there in a public oath that they had done wrong, they proclaimed grandly the merits of the maiden, and dissuading all who heard them from lawless presumption of this kind, they returned to their own homes.

38

Likewise, in declarations of those who speak the truth, wonders are related concerning the spring which (we mentioned before) burst forth where the severed head of the maiden fell to earth. When delicate little children are ill, afflicted with some disease of the body, their cheerful mothers receive them restored suddenly to good health after they have been thrust into the gushing water of this spring and submerged in the swiftness of the stream. It is also commonly known among almost all the inhabitants of Wales that if someone with a fever or one suffering in any limb sprinkles himself with that water or applies the stones bathed by her blood (which we have taught before are found in the brook) to the suffering limb, after the water from the washing of the stones has first been drunk, he will be restored to health immediately. Some people are even urged by divine providence to go there for bathing. Moreover, many come there, very often with the maiden herself urging them through a vision at night, and while returning from there they obtain their wishes.

39

Along the descent of that brook is an excellent mill belonging to the property of the blessed maiden, Winefride, which never ceases to grind on account of any great quantity of rain or snow overflowing it, or any ice, or the troublesomeness of a burning summer drought restricting it. Robbers once went to it and carried off with them the iron implements or instruments by which that kind is used, transferring them to another mill. Truly, while these parts were there, the wheel could not go around nor could any profit come to those officials of the mill. Moreover, the overseers of that function, seeing their trade diminish each day on account of these parts which had been stolen, and no longer enduring their diminution, threw out those parts which they had received from the thieves: immediately, the wheel acquired its freedom to turn the mill, and the other functional instruments followed their old way. The robbers again transferred those castaway parts to other places, where the same things happened in every respect. Finally, understanding that those things were done by divine ordinance, namely that they could not serve to the advantage or gain of any place, they took them back to their proper place, led by repentance and begging forgiveness through the aid of the blessed maiden. In this deed the merits of Saint Winefride and her praises among all the inhabitants of that country were exalted in the highest, and they restrained the bestial madness of the wicked, when all understood that it would go badly for them if ever, enticed by deadly greed, they proceeded against the possessions of the saints.

40

For reasons of this kind, that place in which the blessed maiden, Winefride, had first dwelt has gained the greatest renown. In addition, the prophecy of Blessed Beuno in that place was so powerful that through the blessed maiden, whose first monastic profession was there, the mighty works of God were publicly proclaimed, and many people there found the remedies they wanted for their infirmities. And just as she asked that the place be blessed by God and hallowed by heavenly visitation, so was it afterward shown by clear signs that she had been heard by God on these matters. Indeed, in the display of miracles and in the approbation of wondrous works which happened there it is plainly evident that the aforementioned saint had heralded the truth: it was his prediction that the place would be hallowed by the grace of Heaven, and that God would effect the salvation of many there through the merits of this same maiden. Even today, crowds of faithful people flocking there in troops and returning with joy to their own homes, having obtained what they came for, bear witness to this. And much more copiously do divine mercies occur there for the infirm than in the place where the clay of her most holy body was entombed. I think this has happened for this reason, that she always held that place as her own special one in which the beginnings of her monastic life first shone forth and she was initiated into the divine mysteries, and in which the signs of her martyrdom remain fresh for all time. Nevertheless, divine power works wondrously in both places, and through her aid countless mighty works occur, and desired remedies are granted to the sick. Indeed, sight is restored to the blind through her, and hearing is given to the deaf, and almost all who come there boast that they have obtained their wishes through her, to the praise of Our Lord, Jesus Christ, who with the Father and Holy Spirit lives and reigns for ever and ever. Amen.

TRANSLATION OF THE RELICS

I

Then, after the blessed maiden, Winefride, shining with countless virtues, departed to the heavenly kingdom and many years glided by, while King William was reigning, who first of the Normans ruled in England, Roger, an earl, a man illustrious and conspicuous in all honourableness of morals and piety, began to build a monastery in the city of Shrewsbury. Intending to complete this with diligent care, he added to it at his own expense. Then he installed an abbot and appointed brothers there to serve God. In truth, with the passing of time that place, growing by the mercy of God, benefitted many on the path of salvation, and it offered the fragrance of heavenly perfume to all who dwelt in that country. And although those brothers were strong in virtues, they began to search with intelligent earnestness the things which belong to virtue. Often they complained to one another that they very much lacked relics of the saints, and they turned their attention with the greatest effort to inquiring into this. And since they had heard that the bodies of many saints were preserved in Wales, which was near to them, because this province had been previously inhabited by many saints whose merits were proclaimed in diverse places, they strove in every way to investigate how they might be able to have one of them. Indeed, knowing that they could be protected more by God through the patronage of that one whose honour they might foster on earth by their daily devotion, they tried diligently to be provided with one who might thus be a patron to them. Truly, since many outstanding, most excellent confessors were preserved there, they began to be uncertain about which one they might principally strive after or for whom they might especially wish.

2

Meanwhile, it happened that a certain one of the brothers, seized by a serious sickness, distressed with great grief the rest of the brothers who were pitying him. Full of anxiety for him, they prayed with suppliant souls to God for his safety, humbly asking the monks of neighbouring churches to do the same. In fact, as the great affliction of that brother became known to the monks of the church at Chester, they were equally dismayed in spirit, and they held a procession in the church to beg God for his welfare. While they were prostrate before the holy altar and chanting the Seven Psalms with humble devotion, one of them, Radulph by name, a man of absolutely simple soul who performed the office of sub-prior, fell asleep. And it appeared to him that a most beautiful maiden stood before him and, with a calm countenance, she broke into this speech: "What is the reason for which you are prostrate in prayer?" she said. The monk answered, "A certain brother from our community is tormented by a most grievous illness; we have humbly prostrated ourselves and our prayers before God to pray for his safety." At these words she spoke a second time: "I know that this brother suffers from delirium, but if you truly seek his health, let one of you go to the spring of Saint Winefride and celebrate Mass in her memory in the church which is there. The sick brother will be released immediately." As she said these words, she disappeared. Indeed, the monk returned to himself and, studying in his mind what he had seen and heard, he was unwilling at that time to report the vision to others, fearing that what he had seen would be scoffed at by his companions and considered to be an illusion. And so, after almost forty days had passed, the sick man lay ill on his bed, suffering ever more grievously. Moreover, the rumour was brought to the monks at Chester concerning the most troublesome sickness with which the aforementioned brother was afflicted, and it gave to the other brothers an occasion for speaking about him. Since they were suffering with the sick man and lamenting him in many conversations, the one who had seen the vision took courage and recounted it in order, with all his friends most kindly lending credence to his words, because now understanding that the merits of that maiden would be famous hereafter and knowing that many miracles happened through her, they readily turned their minds to believing what was said, and they trusted the vision. For assuredly they were admonished to go to her spring and to sing a Mass there in her honour; they knew for certain that she was called Saint Winefride, who, they said, had indeed appeared to the aforementioned brother. Therefore, while they were deliberating, two monks were sent to the spring of Blessed Winefride to celebrate Mass in her church, which was next to the spring there, and to pray for the sick man. It came to pass in the same hour in which the Mass was sung that the sick brother at Shrewsbury recovered from his sickness, and he very much cheered his fellow monks on account of his health. After a little time, in fact, the same brother who had been sick was brought to the same place to render thanks to God and the holy maiden for the recovery granted to him. When he had first prayed in the church, and afterward had drunk from the spring and been washed in it, he returned to his monastery, safe and sound in every way. Then the memory of the blessed maiden remained fixed more devoutly in the hearts of the brothers, so that they reckoned they would be happy if they could acquire even a small part of her most holy body. Although they considered that to be hard and difficult, and to exceed their powers, yet they decided straightway that it should be attempted. Knowing that nothing is able to resist God's will, they begged God to be propitious to them and to be their helper; they did not doubt that at His command any impossible or difficult things could easily come to pass for them.

3

At that same time, King Henry, the greatest soldier and friend of peace, guided the defense of the realm. Under his authority, peace and security prevailed in the entire island, and even more, all were allowed to go in peace wherever they wished. Therefore, the aforementioned brothers often sent messengers into Wales, and they steadfastly sought where the more outstanding saints reposed, or preferably, where the grave of the aforementioned maiden was. When the place was found where the bones of the holy maiden, Winefride, were at rest, they rejoiced with great gladness. Then, with the bishop of Bangor (whose diocese was in that province) agreeing with them and promising his help, they brought it about that the leaders and nobles of the country agreed with them and protected them. Proceeding step by step every day, the matter seemed to promise a swift outcome, and it raised the spirits of the brothers in the hope of gaining their ardent wish. But the death of the aforementioned King Henry, occurring unexpectedly, overwhelmed all of Britain with a very great misfortune, and it forced that business to be neglected for a time. Indeed, in the second year of the sovereignty of King Stephen, after disturbances had been checked and the tranquillity of old restored, the abbot of the aforementioned monastery, Herbert by name, with the counsel of his brothers sent his prior, named Robert, into Wales, and a certain monk called Richard was assigned as his companion. Moreover, this same prior, being more solicitous than others in the conduct of this matter, after his emissaries and letters had been despatched often throughout the country, received this in response: that, if he would come himself, he would go back with joy, having obtained his wish. Therefore, he first went to the bishop of the church at Bangor, and sent by him to the prince of that land, he was received kindly enough by him. When he had explained to him the course of his journey and the reason for his coming, the prince answered him in words of this kind: "Indeed, I have not thought that you and your companions have taken up so great a labour without the approval of God and the willingness of the blessed maiden. For, perhaps, seeing that the respect owed her is not rendered by her own people, she desires to be taken elsewhere so that she might receive from strangers the honour which either her own people disdain to give her or neglect to give. Therefore, I willingly comply, and I acknowledge that I assent to her gracious pleasure, lest, resisting, I am compelled to suffer her displeasure in punishment. And though defiled by all uncleanness, the lowest of all men, or worse, yet would I boldly rush to her tomb and, touching her sacred bones, hand them over to you, were it not necessary for me to direct my attention elsewhere in the country for the common good. Both your labours and visions shown to us make clear that she wishes this. Going, therefore, confirmed by leave of my authority, approach the place where the blessed maiden rests; you will find, as I think, some who are opposed to your intention. But, have confidence, because the patronage of the one whose devotion has moved you to take up so great a labour will make them peaceful toward you. Nevertheless, to those men in whose patrimony the body of the aforementioned maiden rests, I shall send an emissary who will make my will known to them and who will make them somewhat more peaceful toward you." When these words had been spoken, he sent them away in peace.

4

And so, when they had gone on from there, they went by a straight way to the place where the most sacred body of the venerable Winefride reposed. All together, there were seven, namely, the aforementioned prior, and with him reverend men: the prior of Chester and a certain priest (a man of many virtues, born of that same nation), and a brother whom the prior had brought with him from his monastery, and three other men. While they were walking innocently along the way and talking about this same matter, they met a man of that country, one who was not of low birth; he asked who the prior of Shrewsbury was. After the prior had been pointed out to him, he spoke these words: "I have come to tell you the message of the men who dwell in that district which is called Guitherin, where the bones of the maiden, Saint Winefride, are preserved. Know that they are stirred by great indignation against you because you are trying to carry off the bodies of saints kept in their possession, to which they and all their own are entrusted. And know for certain that neither fear of the prince nor the threatening of their lords nor desire for any money will make them agree with you in this matter." When these words had been spoken, he left. Indeed, the prior and his colleagues, much saddened on account of these words, were utterly at a loss about what to do or where to turn. Yet, turned to God, they begged with submissive souls that the spirit of counsel be sent to them by Him, and that He who had by a word of command alone calmed the storms of wind and sea might soothe these enmities, and with a humble mind they prayed that He might unite the hearts of those men to themselves. Then, encouraged by the confidence of the Holy Spirit, they continued the journey they had begun. And when they had almost arrived at the place where the blessed maiden's bones were kept, the prior, after deliberation with his brothers, sent two of his companions ahead (namely, the prior of Chester and the aforementioned priest, men well known throughout that country) to provide carefully for everything that they needed.

5

The prior, moreover, remaining that same night at a certain farm with his comrade, was tormented by great anxiety on account of the message that he had heard. And behold, after Lauds had been sung, a certain dignified, honourable person bearing the likeness of a woman appeared to the one attending him, saying these words: "Arise as quickly as possible and tell your lord, after the sorrow and anxiety by which he is troubled has been put aside, to direct his hope to God, knowing that he will depart from here with great joy. Indeed, she for whose love and honour he was sent to this province will bring about her own wish, and she will put him in possession of his desire. Certainly, he will obtain it soon. Then he will return home rejoicing and will make his colleagues glad at his coming." Also, another vision of this kind came to the same prior on that night. A certain abbot of great piety who had been father of the same monastery at Shrewsbury, but who had departed from this life worn-out by old age and full of many virtues, Godfrey by name, appeared to him and released him from the anxieties by which he was distressed, saying, "Do not be faint-hearted, but have faith, because we shall conquer our enemies, and with God's help we shall overcome those who stand opposed to us; know that we shall soon attain what we desire with the greatest devotion." After these words he vanished from his sight. Therefore, from these visions there arose a little confidence in their minds, and the hope of obtaining what they were seeking was restored. Thus, very early in the morning these events began to be reported among them, and they permitted a little cheerfulness in the minds of those hearing them, when suddenly a certain man arrived and increased their confidence concerning the messages of the day before; he advised that they follow him quickly, since God was granting that they should find what they prayerfully desired, and then depart. They immediately mounted their horses and came to that place; after prayers had first been completed, they secretly summoned the priest of that place alone, strenuously entreating him to be a help to them.

6

Truly, the priest listened patiently to their words and gave a response of this kind: "Indeed," he said, "I could have been won over to your wishes by a slight effort, on the one hand because I want to be more closely united to you, and on the other hand because I have long since recognised the will of God and of the maiden in this matter, as I shall show you presently and piously. On the Saturday of the Easter vigil, I was spending the night in prayer in the church that you see here, about to sing the morning hymns, since the time was at hand. After the Psalter had been run through in order, when I took a place for myself on the step before the altar to rest for a little while, I saw a vision which frightened me very much, and which, by threatening, warned me not to stand opposed to you. And, as it seemed, a heavy sleep had not yet overcome me, when a certain most splendid youth exhibiting an angelic countenance stood before me, and he began to shake me, saying: 'Arise!' Indeed, thinking that he was waking me to begin the nocturnal office, I answered: 'It is not yet time for beginning the office. I shall not get up.' He went away, as it seemed to me, and a heavier sleep came over me. And behold, coming a second time and shaking me harder, the same young man said: 'Arise, arise!' Truly, I was unwilling to accede to him and answered as I had before. Covering my head with the cloak that I was wearing, I gave myself over entirely to sleep. A little space of time had intervened when the youth was there again, and he put his hand on the cloak with which I was covered; pulling it from my head with great force and drawing my shoulders up from below, he said a third time: 'Arise, arise, arise, and follow me!' Then I seemed to arise quickly and to follow him instantly. And so we came as far as the tomb of the blessed maiden, Winefride. Pointing that out to me with his finger, he said: 'Note that place carefully, and store away with steadfast recollection the words that I shall say to you. If anyone comes to this place in this year or in the next who wants to remove this stone from here (he was pointing to the layer of marble which was placed over her holy body), beware not to object in any way. But if he wants to take away the very dust from here, likewise yield; do not resist for any reason. Moreover, if he wants to carry off the maiden's bones, do not fight against him, but lend a hand, offering help to him in every way you can. For if you are negligent and found to be a despiser of my words, or if you put off doing what has been divinely made known to you, you will immediately lose your life after this, tormented by a long, lamentable illness.' After these words were spoken, the angelic vision, as I believe it was, disappeared. Therefore, know that with an obliging heart I shall work with you and carefully furnish according to my ability whatever can facilitate your plan. Thus, feeling secure about me, call together the rest of the men and join them to your will by whatever means you can. For truly, with zeal and diligence I shall do what pleases you, and I shall try to subject to your will the minds of those under whose authority this village belongs. And since fortune has brought them before your eyes, say what you want, because they are ready to listen."

7

Then, with that same priest mediating as an interpreter, the prior addressed the band of men that was standing there; he explained to them the reason for his journey, and with persuasive speech he urged them to grant him their approval. Concealing nothing from them about the visions or the other things which had happened, and openly declaring that he had undertaken so great a labour because of the admonition and urging of the maiden herself, he turned them completely to giving him satisfaction. But yet, coming forth suddenly, a certain man, a soldier of Belial, threw the entire assembly into confusion, saying that it was not right that saints be torn away from their native soil and carried off to a country which had nothing to do with them. Even crying out as if he were being attacked by robbers, he said that he could in no way endure this. Indeed, certain ones, silencing his uproar, asked the rest to consult and to respond appropriately with the decision of all after their deliberations. While they were agreeing to this and going off to the council, seeing that the aforementioned man's mind was firmly set on wickedness and that he alone would be an obstacle to them, the prior, with the advice of his brothers, sent a mediator to that man. After money was given, he allied him firmly to himself and sent him back to his own comrades. Truly, the rest, who assented to this simply for the love of God alone, seeing that man suddenly and completely softened, were much astonished; they reckoned that this was done by divine power, and they were even more inspired to carry out what was requested. Therefore, after many roundabout speeches, after countless distinctions of intervening causes, all were of one mind and kindly granted what had been requested. Moreover, offering thanks to God and to them, the prior and his companions asked that the place be shown to them.

8

Furthermore, the place in which so great a treasure is kept is separate from another cemetery where the bodies of those who die now are buried, and it is filled with the bodies of many other saints. Up to this time it has been held in such great awe by the inhabitants of the area that no one dares to be of so great a rashness that he presumes to enter that place except for the sake of prayer. In the middle of it, that is at the head of Saint Winefride, there stands a little wooden church which is frequented by great crowds of people. There is an easy access open to it for all wishing to pray there. Many invalids, many troubled by the afflictions of various diseases enter it to ask for cures for themselves. They do not lament that the cures which they ask for are long delayed, for with health granted to them straightway through the merits of the saints, they return to their own homes safe and sound. No brute animal, no beast of any kind is allowed to come within that cemetery and to live there, for as soon as it has touched the grass that grows over the saints' bodies while it grazes, it falls dead. Indeed, no bold man who enters that place escapes unpunished. In fact, it is reported that two years before the aforementioned brothers had come there, a certain one of the inhabitants of that place, making shoes for himself in the hereditary way from the raw hides of animals, needed laces with which to bind them to his feet. Moreover, in the same courtyard among the saints' tombs there is an oak of wondrous height, untouched from ancient times on account of reverence for the saints. Thinking to make laces for himself from the tender bark of that tree, which is called the rind, the aforementioned man, fearing nothing, seized an axe and hurried to the oak. Raising his hand and striking the tree with the axe, he found something much different than he expected. For when the oak had been struck, it so bound the axe as it struck that it could in no way be moved, and the axe rendered his hand so withered and his arm so inflexible or uncontrollable that the man could in no way bend them to his use. But neither could he withdraw his hand from the axe nor move it in any way. Truly, by a certain divine force the handle of the axe held the man's hand and rendered his whole arm as if dead. And so, pitiably hanging there and crying out with a groaning voice, he suffered tearful punishments for his rashness. A huge crowd of both sexes ran toward his shouting, and seeing him hanging from the axe, many indeed were reduced to tears; moreover, all suffered with him, asking why it happened to him and what was the cause of this kind of misfortune. Indeed, while telling the whole sequence of events in order, he moved all to compassion for him on account of his unusual affliction. When they had admonished him to repent for his offense and confess his guilt and ask pardon, since he had not shown respect to the saints, he began to do this devoutly. Also his parents, prostrate on the ground at the tomb of Saint Winefride, asked amidst tears that she pity him. And since the name of that maiden was more celebrated than the names of the other saints reposing there, and her merits surpassed theirs, they turned to her with heart and body, and prayed for pardon for that transgression. And when all - that man who was suffering and those having compassion on him - said with unanimity, "Saint Winefride, have mercy on him," suddenly through the mercy of God the weak man drew his hand to himself with his arm healed, and the axe fell from the tree. Seeing this, those who were standing there glorified God, and they were more devout in their veneration of the blessed maiden. The oak still stands there as if it were struck recently, teaching that what has been told remains true. From the outcome of this miracle and of many others that are known to have been manifested there, that place is regarded as illustrious and is honoured with great devotion by the inhabitants of the area.

9

Thus, when the brothers mentioned before were led to this place, as they were about to have that for which they had come and to obtain their wish, the aforementioned prior went ahead of his companions by the inspiration of the Holy Spirit, I believe, with no one leading him or showing the way beforehand, and he came by a straight way to Saint Winefride's tomb. And he who had never before been there nor known before the place of the tomb by anyone describing it, entered that churchyard first, with God guiding him, and came straight to the sepulcher of the holy maiden. Standing at the head of the blessed maiden and waiting for his colleagues, as if by a certain divine utterance he was advised inwardly that this was the blessed maiden's sepulcher, and that here he and his colleagues would have what they desired. Indeed, when those who were going to point out the place arrived, they showed him the same one which he had already chosen and at which he was standing. Then, when the laymen had withdrawn, and while the monks and clerics who were present chanted psalms, two of the brothers, namely the prior of Chester and the brother whom we described above that had come with the prior from his monastery, began to dig up the earth with shovels and hoes. A little space of time had intervened, when, after much sweat had been required, almost worn out from their labours, they came to the desired treasure. When this was found, with devout souls they gave thanks to God, and after the bones had been extracted from the dust, as then it was a convenient time for them, they placed them, properly bound, in mantles. And so, saying farewell to those remaining in that district, they began to return home with immense joy.

10

And so, setting out upon their journey, they were going along with cheerful spirits and easing the way with different conversations. Moreover, they inserted one thing frequently among their exchanges of words, that they would prefer it to many vast riches if they could know what was the merit of that which was being carried by them. Neither did God delay long to satisfy their wish in this matter. For, with evening approaching, they were received at a certain trusty inn. Truly, when they were going to bed, a certain sick man in a more remote part of the house began to let out terrible groans and pitiable sounds. Indeed, when the prior asked the cause of that grief, he was told that an ill man was detained there by a very great infirmity of body, and that he would have a great reward from God if he might bring anything to him by which he could be brought to health. Then the prior blessed water that had been brought, and next putting in it a little of the dust found in the blessed maiden's skull, he ordered it to be given to the sick man. Asking that a place to rest be prepared for himself without delay, the man immediately fell asleep. Indeed, arising after a little while, he found himself sound and well, and gave thanks to God and the holy maiden. With their faith strengthened by this miracle, the legates were made happier and more devout in their veneration of the maiden. By many other signs also was it made known to them along the way that what they were bearing was a divine gift.

II

And so, coming on the seventh day to the city of Shrewsbury, from which they had been sent, they dispatched messengers to the monastery to announce that they had what they had gone for. Indeed, when this was heard, the whole community rejoiced much, and declaring that it would be unsuitable for so great a treasure to be received in the monastery without the authority and blessing of the bishop and with a great gathering of people from the entire province, the community determined that the most holy relics should be placed in Saint Giles' church, which is situated at the city gate. This speech pleased all, and they again dispatched the prior to the bishop to confirm by his authority what they were going to do concerning the sacred relic consigned to them by Heaven. Meanwhile, brothers from the convent were assigned to celebrate with devout souls the offices of night and day in the presence of the blessed maiden's body. While they were carefully attending to the things of God and keeping daily vigils with diligent devotion, faithful people came around entrusting themselves to the prayers and merits of the holy maiden. And there was in the same town a certain young man impaired by a very great affliction of body, and he did not have soundness in any of his limbs. Indeed, he was bent over, with his head almost to the ground, and in no way could he raise up his head, but with the functional parts of his whole body lost, he had completely given up hope of sound health. When the rumour was heard about the arrival of the blessed maiden, he ordered a horse to be made ready for him as quickly as possible. Mounted on the horse and held there by the hands of his friends on either side, he was led to the aforementioned church in which the holy relics were being kept. Spending the night there in prayer, at about the end of the night he was troubled by a most sharp pain in his joints. Moreover, resting for a short time early in the morning, after a little while, with day now becoming bright, as the priest was beginning the celebration of Mass, the young man began to grow strong, and after all who were present had long since given up hope, he was restored to his former health. After the gospel, he left the bed on which he had lain all night suffering and proceeded in haste to the altar to present his offering to God and the priest. Then, most devoutly rendering thanks to God and the blessed maiden for the sound health he had received, the young man who had been carried from his parents' house by the hands of others, returned there on his own two feet.

12

This miracle gladdened in great measure the spirits of the community, and, quickly made known throughout the province, moved the minds of those who heard it to awe and reverence. With the passage of every day, the fame and recollection of it increased more, with almost all asking the question about when her translation ought to take place. And so the prior, returning from the bishop and supported by his authority, brought the blessing of God and the bishop to all who were devout in their veneration of the maiden. Then, a day was designated

❧ The Life & Translation of St. Winefride ❧

and announced throughout the assemblies of the neighbouring parishes; all were urged to come on this day who wished to be present at the translation of the venerable saint. Thus, on the appointed day, while the brothers were processing along the way with crosses and candles and a numerous throng of people, the most holy body of the blessed maiden, Winefride, was brought, with all the people genuflecting, and many were unable to refrain from weeping for great joy. In truth, the brothers who had gone to receive the sacred relic learned that divine blessings were shining clearly upon them through the patronage of the blessed maiden, Winefride. Indeed, a pouring rainstorm was copiously drenching the surrounding fields, and the borthers who were going along the way with the precious ornaments of the church were forced to fear not a little lest something be taken away from the honouring of the blessed maiden on account of the threatening rain, and that they might be forced to cease what they had begun to celebrate solemnly with the greatest devotion when it was not at all complete. Their prayerful longings brought to God through the patronage of Saint Winefride deserved to obtain their wish when God in His mercy performed a clear miracle there. For along that entire procession of people going from the monastery to receive the holy relics you might see the rain in the clouds suspended near the earth by divine power, and occasionally individual drops bursting forth toward the earth, indicating in a certain way that they were ready to fall, were held back by the strength of Heaven. All who were there were observing that, with many fearing greatly lest a heavy deluge pour down and force them to scatter in confusion. In fact, many knew that the waters were restrained from falling by divine force, and on that account they venerated the merits of the maiden all the more. Then, after the reception of the holy relics, when the brothers had begun to go back to the monastery, it pleased all that the aforementioned prior who had brought them should address the crowd and instruct everyone about how great were the virtues or what were the merits of the maiden whose translation had taken place there. And when he had done this at length, while the clouds were hovering in the air nearby and threatening their downpour and wetting the surrounding country with their rain, the body of the most holy maiden was received by the brothers with proper reverence while the praises of God were resounding on high. It was brought to the monastery and reverently placed upon the altar which had been built in honour of the holy apostles, Peter and Paul, where, to show the special privilege of the blessed maiden, cures are granted to the sick, and countless miracles happen for the glory and praise of God, to Whom be honour, glory and dominion for ever and ever. Amen.

The Anonymous Life of St. Winefride

Translated by Hugh Feiss, OSB

St. Winefride's Well
Engraving by Samuel & Nathaniel Black
1742

THE ANONYMOUS LIFE OF ST. WINEFRIDE

FIRST PART:
THE STORY OF ST. WINEFRIDE

1.

Here begins the life of St. Winefride, virgin and martyr. It is as salutary to conceal the secret of the king as it is painful not to tell of the wonders of God. For this reason we should begin telling, as is fitting, whatever has been disclosed to us with God's help by the tradition of the ancients regarding Blessed Winefride for the praise of God himself and the merits of his virgin.

In the days when Cadfan[1] ruled over the provinces of Gwynedd, a certain valiant knight, the possessor of only three estates, Teuyth by name, son of Eylud, lived in Tegeingl. These three were called Abeluyc, Maynguen, and Guenphennaun. Teuyth had no children except an only daughter, Winefride by name. From her early years she began to love deeply her heavenly spouse and to reject mortal men. She dedicated her virginity to Him alone. When her father realised this, he was torn between sadness and joy. Sadness, because he had no offspring except her alone, and because – what was even more difficult to bear – she refused to marry a man in order to provide heirs for his patrimony. On the other hand, he was glad that his daughter subjected herself to the reign of God. Because of this grace, the illustrious man proposed to have his daughter trained in the liberal arts.

≫ The Second Life of Winefride of Holywell ≪

2.

While he was entertaining this notion, Blessed Beuno, the abbot, deprived of his dwelling place by the abundance of the sons of Selym, came down to his house. When Winefride's distinguished father realised that Beuno was learned and devout, he consulted with him about his daughter and told him about her desire. Having considered what the knight told him, Beuno said, "If in my hand you will commend to God your estate, I will dwell here with you and teach your daughter the divine law." Teuyth responded to this, "Lord, if this were in my power, no one would be more eager than I to grant what you request. But, as it is, servant of God, if it does not seem too long to you, I want you to stay here until I receive the king's response to this matter." Beuno replied, "Dearest son, proceed. May God precede you so you may successfully conclude your business." So Teuyth, leaving his house for the house of the king, sought the palace of his lord. There he asked resolutely that he endorse what he had decided regarding his patrimony. He replied, "O worthy man, it is not up to me or you to separate your estate from the rest of the province if to do so would be useless to it or to my need. However, if it pleases you, whichever of these three estates you choose I grant to you freely for divine service, provided you leave me the other two."

3.

Having heard this excellent reply of the king, he went back home so he could report what he had heard from the king to Beuno, "Therefore, if you wish to remain with me," he said, "choose for the service of God whatever place in my patrimony seems best suited." Blessed Beuno said, "I choose to have my dwelling in the solitude of Beluyc." And so it was done. Beuno, with the patronage of Teuyth, located his hut in a ravine which in the language of the Britons is called Sechnant. He built a small church there in which he celebrated Mass. Each day he taught the sacred scriptures to the virgin Winefride. Teuyth and his household attended mass each day at the place where Beuno offered the celebration.

4.

At that time, it happened on a certain Sunday that Teuyth was there with his wife to hear Mass while Winefride had been delayed at her father's house, because she was to bring the things necessary for mass; that is, fire and water with salt. Meanwhile, Caradog, son of Alauc, who was sprung from a royal line, was tired out from hunting wild animals. He approached the house, for he was anxious to have a drink because he was thirsty. When he arrived there, he inquired about the whereabouts of the owner of the villa, for he had some secret which he was anxious to disclose. The girl, who was in the house alone, hurried to meet the one who was asking for her father. She greeted him politely and said that her parents had gone to hear the preaching of Beuno at mass.

Caradog saw the young lady's clear and rosy countenance, and he admired how she was well-formed in her body and her face. His heart began to burn with a desire for her which engulfed it. Finding her alone in the house without any witnesses, he forgot his thirst, so great was his love. He said to her, "O dearest virgin, agree to my plans by granting the intimacy of suitors, for I desire you passionately." To these things the virgin replied, "My Lord, what utterance is this of a man so highborn as you to a handmaid so common as I? Sir, I cannot to do this. I am betrothed to another man, whom I soon must marry." When he heard this, Caradog was furious. He said, "Stop talking this irritating and meaningless nonsense and agree to have sex with me. Agree to marry me and I will make you my wife." When the girl saw that the mind of the man was overwhelmed with passion, she took action to avoid being overpowered by the man's violence. She said,

"Grant me, Lord, to go into my clothes room so that, wearing the proper clothes, I can more suitably embrace you. Since it is necessary, I will abandon the service enjoined on me, and I will be subject to your will." Caradog answered the girl, "If there is no tarrying, it will not seem too much for me to wait for you a little while."

5.

Having received this permission, the girl went through the bed chamber and ran to the valley, trying to escape as quickly as possible from the man's line of vision. Caradog realised that he had been tricked by the virgin's ingenuity. He was furious and pounded his spurs on his horse's flanks in an effort to capture the girl. The girl stayed ahead of the man until she arrived at the door of the monastery, where she hoped for the peaceful protection of God and Beuno. But as she lifted her foot over the threshold, the man caught up to her with a sword and cut off her head.

6.

When her parents saw this, they fell into a swoon for a while. When they returned to themselves, they wept miserably. When Beuno saw this disaster, he was overcome with a great sadness. Leaving the altar, he approached the door quickly in order to learn who had done this slaughter. Raising his eyes, he beheld cruel Caradog still standing with the bloody sword in his hand. When he realised Caradog had done it, he cursed him on the spot. Instantly before his eyes, Caradog melted like a burning candle. Then Beuno returned to the body. To the body which was lying outside he rejoined the head which had been hurled inward by the blow from the sword. Then he prayed earnestly to God, asking God to vivify the body so that the enemy would not gloat over it. As soon as he prayed, the body received back its soul with its power. There was no mark visible on it except a slight scar on her neck. The place stained with her blood cracked and a turbulent fountain gushed out and watered it. Its rocks still seem as bloody today, as they did on that first day. The moss smells like incense, and it cures various illnesses.

7.

When Beuno saw that God had worked such a miracle for her sake, he said to her in the hearing of her parents, "My Sister, God has destined this place for you. I need to go elsewhere, to a place God will provide for me to stay. However, do this for me each year about this time. Send me a cloak of your own making." "My Lord," she said, "in my heart there is no resistance to granting you this, but to me it seems that will be very difficult for it to reach you. I don't know where you are going to live." The saint said to her, "Do not worry about that. A stone stands in the middle of the fountain's flow. On it I have been accustomed to repeat my prayers. Put your cloak on it as prearranged. Then let it come to me, if it will." So, after a mutual blessing, they separated.

8.

Blessed Winefride lived in this hermitage for many days of her life as Beuno had advised her to do. Moreover, each year, on the vigil of John of the Baptist, she sent the cloak to Beuno in the following way. She arranged it upon that rock. The rock, submerged in the fountain's stream, carried it, dry inside and out, all the way to the sea, and through the sea to the port of Sachlen and to Beuno. Thus did Beuno receive the gift of the virgin each year. Through the virgin's merit, the power of this cloak was such that when Beuno was sheltered in it, rain could not drench him, nor could the wind dishevel his hair. Because of this, Beuno was called "dry cloak."

9.

People remember that once she set out for Rome in order to visit the places of the holy apostles and there to offer herself devoutly and completely to God in the presence of the relics of the saints. When the trip was over, she returned to her former desert. In those days, all the saints of Britain were called to the synod of [Whitby].[2] To it came blessed Winefride with the other saints. There all things were arranged devoutly according to the synodal process; namely, that the saints who previously had lived dispersed and alone, having no rule but their will, would henceforth come together in suitable places and amend their way of life under prefects appointed for them. Whence it happened that Winefride was chosen for eleven virgins so that they would receive from her a model of a holy way of life.

This virgin was distinguished by such eloquent knowledge that it is beyond our power to describe. The words she uttered were thought by her listeners to be sweeter than honey and more nourishing than milk. Hence by all she was publicly called White Winefride. She spoke with the splendour of wisdom and lived resolutely. The place where she lived with her virgins is called Gwytherin. And there, when her life ended in the sleep of death, she was buried with her virgin companions on the 8th day of the calends of July. She rests in Christ, to whom there is honour and glory forever. Amen. Thus ends the life of Holy Winefride, virgin and martyr.

The Second Life of Winefride of Holywell

PART TWO:
THE MIRACLES WHICH OCCURRED AT ST. WINEFRIDE'S WELL

10.

Here begin her miracles. We have given accounts of some of these known to the local inhabitants or seen by them, which seem worthy of retelling. From the day on which the spring began to flow where the blood of the martyr had poured out, a miracle unheard of through the centuries, wondrous to retell and stunning to hear, occurred in the middle of the bubbling fountain. Three very clear little stones, rising and falling in the rushing spring, took turns being on the top, middle and bottom, the way knives[3] thrown by a skilled juggler alternate. This went on for many years. At the time when Danes in Tegeingl were subject to the Britons, a certain unfortunate woman went down to the well and saw the pebbles playing before her. She was seized with greed for them and grabbed one. At that the other two disappeared. Then she went home and was seized by a sudden illness. After a few days, she died. She confessed before her death and returned the pebble. However, what had happened before was seen no longer. My brothers, it is not surprising how the stones confirmed the power of the martyr, since we read that the holy fathers carried rocks in testimony to them.

11.

Another time it happened that a man, accused of theft, committed perjury on the spring and the sacred precincts of the martyr's church. In due time it became known how the blessed virgin felt about those who presumed to do a forbidden act. A goat which the man had eaten uttered a horrible bleating from inside the stomach of the thief, and so it was clear that he was guilty. This is a horrible event: what was denied by the oath of a rational animal was disclosed by a brute animal and, what is more astounding, by one that was already eaten. It leaves no doubt that the Lord works wonders for his saints, for he is utterly wonderful in all his saints [Ps 67.36].

12.

Likewise, in the days of the French in that same land, a deserved revenge was effected by God through the same martyr. A certain matron turned against her handmaid because of fierce jealousy. She wounded the girl with sharp blows. When the girl fled to the shrine for sanctuary, she continued beating her fiercely. When the unfortunate maid reached the church and tried to enter, she found the door fastened shut. She had hoped to find sanctuary in the basilica; now she didn't know what to do. She clung to the door. Meanwhile the matron did not spare her any of her beating. The martyr of the Lord saw the violence aimed at her. She felt compassion for her shame and misery. She immediately obtained vengeance from the Lord. Then the captive, who had been continually lacerated for a long time and was now prostrate under the matron's feet, arose, as God wished, and butted her head against the cheek of her mistress who was leaning over her. The force of the blow separated her cheek from her skull, and her throat was twisted back toward the other ear. She remained deformed like this until the day she died. It was fitting that she, who would not stop inflicting blows until she had snuffed out the spirit, should not cease being corrected until the separation of her body and soul. So it is that those who have not venerated God and the tabernacles of the saints find their faces filled with disgrace.

13.

Again, after some time had passed, the law of peace had been violated throughout the country. With the French and the Welsh fighting each other, innumerable robbers from Gwynedd depopulated all Tegeingl. They sent eight sacrilegious men to despoil even the dwelling of the virgin, Winefride, and its estate. They rushed there and even snatched away with them the animals tied to the wall of the church. However, they weren't able to take pleasure from this for very long. They suffered a horrible death shortly afterwards. The leaders in this wickedness, the ones who had organised it, were cut down by an abominable death before a year had passed. What shall I tell you? Hardly one of that great multitude or of those associated with them escaped.

Because zeal for the house of the Lord consumed him, they were cast down while they were raised up [Ps 68.10].

14.

In those same days, a certain deacon of the same church was taking home on his horses the tithes of a certain village of his parish. The deacon had sacred ornaments hanging from his neck for protection. When he had come across the boundary of the martyr's estate, he chanced to fall in among robbers. They had no respect either for the martyr or for sacred things. They robbed him and forced him to go with them as they took their spoils away, although he pleaded with them to be merciful toward him for the sake of God and God's martyr. When they had taken him a long way away, by God's and the martyr's will, it occurred to him to flee. When he undertook to do so, the leader of the robbers pursued him on foot. Finally, this one who was seeking to capture him was overtaken by a disaster. He was pierced in the leg by his own lance. He lost the nerves in his leg and could no longer proceed. Because this one was punished in his body, all the rest were corrected in their minds. The deacon, giving thanks to God and the martyr for his liberation, returned home safe and sound with his things.

The Lord certainly sends his angel in the midst of those who fear him and frees them [Ps 33.8]. Such as have no fear of the Lord and his saints before their eyes find their wickedness a thing hateful to them [Ps 35.3]. It descends on their heads [Ps 17.7].

15.

At the same period, a certain French knight, the possessor of the same estate, was measuring out a mill on the bank of the spring and began to dam up the water. When the knight saw that the water gushed out toward Beuno's rock which was near the pond in the middle of the river, he commanded that it be placed within the pond. However, although one hundred yoke of oxen were brought, it would not rise from its spot. It remained immobile as though it had solid roots, and it could not be torn out. Later the knight, thinking that his workers had acted deviously, forced them to try again and again. Thinking that he could roll out the rock with nothing more than his foot, he became enraged and kicked the rock. But immediately the nerves in his knee were bent back and became stiff. He was crippled for the rest of his life.

At the same time, with bold daring, the wife of this knight entered across the edge of the fountain. Because it is especially for the sick, she bathed there unlawfully. Alas, this too was not unpunished. She remained sterile for the rest of her life. She grieved before all. It was fair that those who encroached on the inheritance of the martyr and unlawfully polluted her sanctuary would afterwards be for all those in the neighbourhood an object of mockery and scoffing, insult and disgrace [Ps 78.4]. The virgin of the Lord was renowned for these miracles and innumerable others, yet more wondrous, worked against the perverse. If all were handed down and remembered in writing, time would run out before the supply of words. For now let these suffice regarding the punishment of evildoers, lest they delight in doing anything wicked against the rights of the virgin, for next we need to turn our plow to making furrows elsewhere in order to make known the benefits of the virgin toward the sick.

16.

In the time of the French, in the same region, there was a certain rich man who was ill. He was in control of much money but not of himself. Hearing the fame of the virgin, he headed there as quickly as he could, conveyed in a cart. Arriving at the memorial of the blessed virgin, he dispersed all his possessions to the church and to the poor and thus made himself a poor man. He found no more delight in things of the world, but trusted in the Lord. After he had washed three times in the water of the font and finished three nights of vigil and praying in the church, you could hear then and there in a wondrous way a creaking in his feet and legs and arms. Those bones, which from birth until then had been unseemly bent and contracted against his buttocks, now stretched out so that their joints were in the proper place. You can imagine that there and then you could have seen a happy crowd of bystanders, thanking God and the virgin. You would indeed! How just was this recompense! The one who had deprived himself of his financial substance received the substance of his own body endowed with all its senses and strength. He distributed what he had loved; he found what he had always wanted. Thus, one who came in a wagon because he lacked the use of his feet, left using his own feet fully and completely healed.

17.

A certain man, led to do penance for his crimes, was wrapped in iron bindings for many years. His arms were miserably lacerated with the rusty iron by the time he came to the sanctuary. He spent the night in vigils and prayers and at dawn went to the well. As he washed his hands and extended his arms into the spring, it seemed to him that two delicate hands loosened the chains from his arms. Brothers, who can doubt that the virgin was present there at that moment? The man had come from the church to the spring bound, and he returned from the spring to the church unbound, thanking God and God's martyr. As a sign, he hung up those very chains, which for many years have been hanging there on view as an offering. Ponder, men and women alike, how this virgin and martyr of the Lord is to be honoured by all with veneration and reverence, for clearly she helps those who call to her.

18.

Nor should one fail to mention what she did for a certain man afflicted with dropsy, who could scarcely be dragged into her hands. When he had kept vigils and washed in the waters of the spring, she freed him from the excessive humour, so that only the amount of that humour proper to human nature remained.

19.

A epileptic felt the hand of the martyr no less. According to custom he was led to the basilica, where he passed the night in vigil and prayer. A wondrous thing happened to him, for he suffered two attacks but in neither case was he harmed. At twilight he felt the epilepsy to be coming on him so he ran quickly to the church. When the name of the Lord and his martyr had been invoked over him by the priests, the evil which had begun immediately left him. Another day, at dawn, as the illness in him became more acute, he was put into the well, and thereafter it never attacked him again.

Similarly, two boys, brothers, were cast into the well when the same illness invaded them and were completely cured. Many, indeed, numberless, others suffering from the same disease were cured. In fact, they say that the virgin especially cures this sickness of epilepsy with the power of her merits, although she cures others as well. No illness is worse than this one, which deprives one of consciousness, gnaws away the heart, practically vomits up the soul, strikes the brain, bites the tongue, foams, roars, twists the members, and destroys one totally. Because it is so awful, she strives especially to cure it.

20.

A woman brought with her to the memorial of the blessed martyr a boy, her son, who was mute from birth. When she had celebrated the solemn services of vigils, she washed him in the spring and put water into his mouth. She heard her son speaking proper words and asking for his clothes. When they saw this, those present were awe-struck. They glorified God and the martyr, while giving their congratulations to the mother.

21.

Another time some crippled youths, comrades, went down into the spring together. But only one was granted health, because he believed firmly. When he descended and his members stretched out, he let out a horrible yell which stunned the ears of those standing nearby or even at some distance who heard it, for the power of the Lord can never remain hidden when it goes out from Him at the intercession of the saints.

22.

A certain boy, who thought his limbs were useless because they had little feeling in them, immediately received the steadfast[4] largesse of the virgin. By her prayers she reestablished all his limbs in a healthy state.

23.

A certain man born blind, after having attended the liturgy in the shrine of the martyr, went to the spring and washed. He began to see and gave thanks.

24.

Two boys, suffering from the stone, petitioned the virgin. Their natural digestion was restored. One of these two who were freed from their illness was immediately inebriated with the charism of the prophetic muse.

25.

In a similar fashion, many gnawed on by worms all the way to their innermost parts experienced the help of the virgin. The worms were killed, and the people returned home cured.

Some mentally incompetent, troubled by unclean spirits, biting with their teeth and uttering vain words, were led there with difficulty in chains, but they returned home from there fully in control of their reason and themselves. Frequently cured, also, were those running fevers who waited for her gracious love. She cured fevers of every sort with the ointment of the sacred font.

Many times this most kind virgin cures those with dropsy, restores the paralyzed, heals those with gout, and cures the melancholy. Equally she removes sciatica, roots out cancer, tones down madness,[5] and removes haemorrhoids. She cures persistent coughs, expels

❧ The Second Life of Winefride of Holywell ❧

stomach aches and discharges, dissolves obstructed menstruation which causes sterility, and blocks excessive and immoderate blood. Why should I try to explain all by listing a few? The benefits rendered by the virgin are so many and so great that their infinity blocks any finite explanation. But that I may summarise all briefly: from her shrine she quickly helps, lovingly and kindly and without any delay, all those who are suffering from any weakness, illness or disease or any infirmity when, with pure faith, they ask for the martyr's intercession with God. Thus she fully restores the senses and strength of each.[6]

26.

Nor should what happened regarding the spring of this same virgin, after the expulsion of the French from the whole of Gwynedd, be hidden in the silence of Lethean forgetfulness. The spring of the martyr appeared to flow with a milky liquid for three days. At dawn on the first of those days it had the colour and taste of milk. A priest who was going out early in the morning from matins (which was celebrated liturgically in the church of the same martyr near to this excellent spring) saw what was happening and ran to it quickly, carrying with him a bottle which he filled and kept carefully and diligently. Then when he ran back with a sponge in order to fill it also, the liquid had lessened somewhat in luster. Thus for three days it gradually lost the colour and taste of milk and took on its former appearance.

Lest anyone think that this occurred because of the force of the winds or unseasonable rain, he should know that not for some time before or after was there any disturbance of the elements. Nor should any hesitation or doubt arise, because the inhabitants say that this often happened. The liquid, received by the priest and transmitted everywhere to the sick to be drunk, healed them and so conferred on them the assistance which the virgin was accustomed to offer. And well did her spring appear to be of sweet savour since it was of one who, called White Winefride, showed herself to be kind, soft, meek, sweet, loving, gentle, well-disposed, pleasant, and merciful to those asking her favours.

27.

In no way should one despise what this virgin did on behalf of a little girl. Toward evening one day, a man carried the lifeless corpse of a girl with him to the shelter of the martyr so that it could be buried. When the priest saw that night was falling, he postponed the burial until morning. He firmly locked the doors of the church, leaving inside the body which, rigid with deadly cold, was wrapped in a cloth and bound with bandages. When the priest entered the church at the first light of dawn to celebrate vigils according to his regular practice, he found the girl now alive. She was freed from the bandages and cloth, but was still sitting and pulling herself along with her palms because of her weakness. She bore no mark of death on her. She asked him for hospitality and food. With gratitude he gave thanks to God and to the martyr. What wonder if she calls the dead back to life with her prayer, when she herself once dead had come back to life?

28.

We should call to memory what we omitted above regarding the correction of evildoers. At different times two clerics had committed sacrilege within the precincts of the virgin. One of them was taking away a portable book when he was suddenly caught in the theft. Because a workman is worthy of his pay, he was punished with a whipping. The other, having stolen a missal, offered it everywhere and to everyone for sale, but found no one who would trade with him. Finally by God's will he returned and, no longer able to conceal his sacrilege, he was hanged as he deserved.

The Second Life of Winefride of Holywell

29.

God, who alone works wonders, does not cease to work these miracles here for his virgin and martyr Winefride, either to help the kindly or to punish the impious. God in perfect Trinity lives and reigns, one for all ages.

Here ends the Passion of St. Winefride, virgin and martyr, on the 8th day of the calends of July (June 22).

Notes

1. Latin: *Katuanus*. My choice of translations for Welsh names is eclectic. In this case, I follow A.W. Wade-Evans, *Vitæ sanctorum et genealogiæ* (Cardiff, 1944) 288–309, from whose transcription and translation of this life I have profited in several places.
2. The Latin has "of Winefride", but that does not seem to make sense.
3. The Latin has *"more artanorum a iaculatore proiectorum"*. This should be emended to *"artavorum"*, "little knives."
4. Here I follow the correction of the Acta Sanctorum: *"inolitam"*.
5. The Latin text has *"disnoim"*. I have adopted the meaning suggested in the *Acta Sanctorum*. Wade-Evans has "shortness of breath".
6. My translation of *"utriusque hominis"* is deliberately ambiguous. The author may have had in mind something like "inner person" and "outer person". Wade-Evans translates as "pertaining to either sex".

Winefride's Well-Cult

by Catherine Hamaker

St. Winefride's Well
1830

WINEFRIDE'S WELL-CULT

> ... *the very ground stained by her blood split open, and a boiling spring gushed forth, drenching that spot. Even to this day these stones can be seen, bloodstained just as they were that first day. The moss there smells of incense, and cures many diverse ailments ...*

Thus Winefride's biographer describes her holy well, springing forth at the very spot where her severed head fell to the ground. This well in turn became the focus for Winefride's miracle-working cult throughout the Middle Ages and long afterward. While it is one of the most popular well-sites in Wales, well cults and water veneration hold an important place in British religious life.

The prevalence of holy springs as essential features of British saints' shrines would seem to suggest some sort of pagan connection, and in fact many Celtic historians presume this to be the case. Speaking of the holy wells and springs of Ireland, one historian states that they are "doubtless the Christianised descendants of places of pagan pilgrimage;"[1] Francis Jones, in his 1992 work, *The Holy Wells of Wales*, asserts likewise. But is this supportable from the anthropological and archaeological evidence available?

Since the debunking of Margaret Murray's work on the topic during the 1970s, close scrutiny has been paid to the topic of paganism in Britain – in both the ancient and mediæval periods. Unfortunately, at least for the pre-Roman era, a scarcity of evidence makes almost any statement about so-called "Celtic Paganism" conjecture rather than fact. Burials and grave goods comprise the bulk of the archaeological record; few pre-Roman architectural structures survive in Wales, and none of them are associated with holy wells or churches. One site, at Lydney in Gloustershire, shows evidence of a shrine to Nodens, a pagan god who supposedly was himself the object of pre-Christian pilgrimage devotion; unfortunately, this example does not tie in neatly as a site of later Christian worship.[2] The offerings at this shrine do have a familiar ring for students of a later period – in addition to coins and jewelry, small models of human body parts were offered to the god as a request for healing of the afflicted area. This is echoed in the later mediæval period, when wax models of body parts were placed at healing shrines for this same purpose.[3]

It does seem certain that wells and springs were thought to be special places by pagans of both Gallic and Roman origin. Several excavations of British wells have yielded a quantity of offering-type artifacts, including animal bones and on rare occasion human remains. A large pre-Christian ritual offering of bones, weapons, tools, and chains was discovered at Llyn Cerrig Bach in Anglesey; while there is little concrete evidence of pagan temples associated with bodies of water, many river names (such as the Dee in North Wales) derive from the name of a patron deity.[4] Rivers such as the Thames contain numerous "offering" items from the pre-Christian period, suggesting that water itself held some sort of divine association for British pagans. Roman paganism held similar beliefs; the hot springs at Bath are famous for their collection of offered items – particularly the prayers and curses inscribed on lead sheets which were then thrown into the springs. These items, perhaps more than any others, make clear for us a pagan concept of the spring as a connection with the otherworld. Celtic literature is filled with references to wells, lakes, or rivers as boundaries between the material and spirit world, and the Romans often built temples at or near sacred springs.[5] Offerings made into water disappear from view and can thus be thought to have been "received" by the gods, who might then be inclined to look favourably upon the offerer. This is not a concept unique to Britain, or even to areas touched by Roman paganism.

E. Sidney Hartland cites examples of similar practices from all over the world, and suggests that traditions of placing personal objects in holy wells "are to be interpreted as acts of ceremonial union with the spirit identified with [the] well ..."[6]

It is not hard, then, to make the leap in suggesting that the British mediæval fondness for dedicating wells to holy figures is traceable to a longstanding tradition of water veneration. Many of the traditions concerning Welsh wells collected by folklorists in the last two centuries have a distinctly un-Christian flavor – particularly the traditions of divination using saints' wells.[7] Excavation of the River Thames has unearthed a large number of mediæval pilgrims' badges at a ferry crossing.[8] Thrown into the river as a supplication for safe passage? Perhaps. While true "paganism" did not exist as a discrete entity alongside the Christian majority, the Christianity of Britain preserved pagan traditions in its native population by appropriating them to itself. Pope Gregory's plan for the Christianisation of Britain, stated in a letter written in 601 AD and quoted by Bede, lends support to the idea that this was the result of deliberate forethought:

> ... we have been giving careful thought to the affairs of the English, and have come to the conclusion that the temples of the idols among that people should on no account be destroyed. The idols are to be destroyed, but the temples themselves are to be aspersed with holy water, altars set up in them, and relics deposited there.[9]

It is important to emphasise, however, that the Church's efforts were aided by a populace pre-disposed to think of certain places and types of geographic features as spiritually significant.

Keeping this in mind, we can see that Winefride's well itself is hardly unique – the British Isles are dotted with over seven thousand sacred springs and wells, mostly concentrated in the traditionally Celtic areas of Scotland, Ireland, Wales, and Cornwall.[10] Unlike many

⟩⟨ Winefride's Well-Cult ⟩⟨

of these wells, however, Winefride's possessed a very specific connection with its saint – the legend linking the rise of the spring with the fall of the saint's head. Stories of decapitation occur fairly frequently in mediæval Welsh literature and hagiography, though the saints involved often recover from the experience. One who did not, St. Justinan, has a vita which bears some similarities to Winefride's, the most obvious one of which being that a spring arises at the site of his decapitation. Unluckily for Justinan, he has no miracle-working confessor to restore him to life, as did Winefride. He does however manage to pick up his head and stride from the site of his murder to the site where he wishes his tomb to be built before actually dying. John of Tynemouth's fourteenth century account of Justinan's life describes the spring as "a copious fountain of clearest water ... whose stream, quaffed by sick folk, conveys health of body to all." Miracles at both Justinan's well and tomb are recounted by Tynemouth; this, along with the Lives of St. Winefride included in this volume, are the only Welsh saints' vitæ I have found which follow this pattern of healing well advertisement. Justinan never achieved the level of widespread popularity which Winefride enjoyed; his well was merely one of the many satellite sites surrounding St. David's cathedral in southwest Wales, and no doubt attracted few pilgrims independent of this association.

Though Winefride's bones were translated from her burial place to the monastery at Shrewsbury in the twelfth century, the cult continued to operate at Holywell despite this.[11] Some relics of hers remained in Gwytherin, housed in a tent-shaped reliquary in the Irish style which was seen and drawn by Edward Lhwyd in 1698. This reliquary was slowly dismantled over the centuries; an eighteenth-century source mentions the wooden casket but omits mention of its ornate metalwork covering seen in Llwyd's drawing, which suggests that it might already have been removed by this time. In the early nineteenth century, Samuel Lewis' *Topographical Dictionary of Wales* stated that a wood chest which had formerly contained Winefride's relics was still preserved at Gwytherin.[12] In 1844, Father John Griffith Wynne S.J., on a pilgrimage to Gwytherin, was told by a clerk at the site that the box which had held the saint's relics had been largely demolished by devout visitors, who paid a shilling apiece for bits of the chest to take home with them. Wynne himself took part of one of the end boards, and later presented it to St. Winefride's Church at Holywell. This fragment was long thought lost or destroyed; but it came to light in 1991, still in the church where Wynne had originally deposited it.[13] From this fragment it is possible to date the reliquary (also called the Arch Gwenfrewi) to the mid-8th century, and it is thus the oldest surviving physical evidence of a Welsh saint's formal cult.[14]

Despite this evidence of early local veneration for St. Winefred, her popularity was apparently of limited scope until the later mediæval period. Holywell was granted to the monks of St. Werberg in 1093, and in 1240 Dafydd ap Llewellyn gave the land to nearby Basingwerk Abbey. Yet Giraldus, with his penchant for local trivia, makes no mention of Holywell or miracles performed there in his *Itinerary*. Archbishop Baldwin's entourage stopped the night at Basingwerk during their whirlwind tour of North Wales, but apparently Winefred was deemed unworthy of mention by Giraldus in his description of the area.[15] Admittedly, the journey around North Wales was far shorter than the time spent in South Wales and Giraldus himself was likely more familiar with the southern localities and landmarks. The fact that Holywell is not mentioned at all in the Itinerary suggests to me, however, that Winefred the miracle-working saint had at this time not gained the international reputation that she was later to enjoy.

The late Middle Ages saw a dramatic surge of interest in female saints, no doubt in reaction to the growing popularity of the Marian cult in both Britain and on the continent. "Home-grown" virgin saints were the subject of much devotional activity in Wales, especially in the north; the shrines of St. Dwynwen in Anglesey and St. Melangell in the Berwyn mountains gained renewed attention in this period, and St. Winefride's well became a rival to St. David's cathedral in its reputation as a pilgrimage site.

When her well's miraculous powers gained fame in England, Holywell attracted a number of celebrity pilgrims.[16] Richard I was forced to hide out at Basingwerk when attacked en route to pay tribute to St. Winefride. By the fourteenth century, her cult in Shrewsbury had increased such that a new shrine was built for her relics, and the bones of her confessor St. Beuno were brought to Shrewsbury to be installed in the wall of the church; a fine was levied on the abbey for the theft of Beuno's relics, but they stayed in Shrewsbury nonetheless.[17] Adam of Usk states that in 1416 Henry V "with great reverence went on foot in pilgrimage from Shrewsbury to St. Winefride's Well in North Wales."[18] Edward IV also went there on pilgrimage, and Richard III granted the abbot of Basingwerk an annuity for the purpose of maintaining a priest at the shrine.[19]

Winefride's chronicler recounts numerous miracles at her well; a man who has stolen and eaten a goat is given away by its bleatings from within his stomach; a woman who beats her serving girl becomes horribly deformed when the girl appeals to St. Winefride for assistance; a knight who dams up the stream that flows from the well is permanently lamed.[20] Lest we think that this saint is perhaps a touch on the vindictive side, the chronicler quickly adds an endorsement for her healing abilities that reads like the back of a patent medicine bottle. The chapel at Holywell was built directly over the well itself; offerings of rags, pins, buttons and coins were dropped directly into the spring,[21] and the interior of the chapel was hung with crutches and other souvenirs left by many thankful pilgrims.[22]

WINEFRIDE'S WELL-CULT

At the time of the Reformation, the Welsh saints' shrines were dismantled with the same bombastic zeal as were those of their English brethren; relics were scattered, statues burnt, and sacred images obliterated. Needless to say, pilgrimages to holy sites were forbidden by the new church as superstitious acts of a foolish populace. But while the outward trappings of the saints' cults could be removed, altered, or destroyed, the holy wells remained as a mute testament to the shrines' existence. Pilgrims continued to come to the wells to make offerings and pray for healing miracles even after the Reformers had left their mark.

By the sixteenth century, Winefride's chapel and well were so well-known in both Wales and England that they escaped destruction by Reformist officials. The well-shrine had enjoyed a tremendous vogue in the early sixteenth century, and reported an income of about £10 per year. After the Dissolution, the new Church was quick to see the financial advantage of maintaining the shrine in its former condition. The leaser of the property in 1535 lodged a complaint with the Court of Augmentations stating that "bold Catholics" had begun to stand at the shrine and exhort pilgrims not to drop offerings into the well, as the King's men would soon fish the money out again. Rather, supplicants were asked to put coins into special boxes provided by the bold Catholics themselves.[23] Winefride's shrine was the most lucrative pilgrimage site in Wales at this time; its income of offerings was estimated to be at least £10 a year, and perhaps a good deal more. (The next most popular site, the shrine to the Virgin Mary at Pen-Rhys in South Wales, was a distant second with an estimated £6 per annum.)[24]

Winefride remained popular as a healing saint throughout the sixteenth and seventeenth centuries; the shrine attracted the attention of Protestants as being a Catholic stronghold. According to a Privy Council document of 1629, on St. Winefride's day of that year nearly fifteen hundred "gentlemen and gentlewomen of divers countries" were assembled at Holywell to pay homage to the saint. The Catholic King James II and his queen made a pilgrimage to Holywell in 1686, in hopes of gaining the saint's aid in conceiving a male heir.[25]

St. Winefride continues to be known for her healing powers down to the present day. Philip Metcalf's 1712 translation of Winefride's Life recounts numerous contemporary incidents of miraculous healing at the well; in an appendix to a 1922 reprinting of Metcalf's work, Rev. Herbert Thurston recounts a number of documented cures from the eighteenth and nineteenth centuries. He concludes with the story of a young woman with a tubercular knee, who was cured at St. Winefride's well in 1914. In addition to a first-person account by the woman concerning her miraculous cure, Thurston presents a note written by one of the sisters at the hospice at Holywell, informing the woman's parish priest of the miracle, and a brief letter from the woman's doctor to the author which attests to both the condition of her knee before the cure, and to the fact that she is fully restored to health at the time of the letter's writing (1916).[26] Obviously, the allure of St. Winefride and her well is hardly a thing of the distant past. Her shrine today attracts both pilgrims and tourists, though the well is only a shadow of its former self due to changes in the water table provoked by the advent of the industrial age. Of all the many sacred springs and wells in Britain, few have displayed the enduring popularity that marks the site at Holywell; St. Winefride stands out among her fellow "well-saints," both for her continued efficacy and her tenacity during the Reformation and in subsequent centuries.

NOTES

1. Barry Raftery, *Pagan Celtic Ireland: The Enigma of the Irish Iron Age* (London: Thames and Hudson, 1994) 182–183.
2. Wade H. Richards, "Settlement Studies in Dark Age Wales" *Comitatus* 17 (1986) 83.
3. Ronald Hutton, *The Pagan Religions of the Ancient British Isles* (Oxford: B. Blackwell, 1991) 245.
4. Janet Bord and Colin Bord, *Sacred Waters: Holy Wells and Water Lore in Britain and Ireland* (London: Granada, 1985) 4–7.
5. Mara Freeman, "Sacred Waters, Holy Wells" *Parabola* 20 (1995) 53–54.
6. E. Sidney Hartland, "Pin Wells and Rag Bushes" *Folklore* 4 (1893) 469.
7. For some examples, see Elissa Henken, *Traditions of the Welsh Saints* (Cambridge, D.S. Brewer, 1987) 228–229; Bord and Bord, 43–45; and Hartland, 452–453.
8. Hutton, 292.
9. Bede, *A History of the English Church and People*, translated by Leo Shirley-Price (London: Penguin, 1968) 86.
10. Bord and Bord, 24.
11. Glanmor Williams, *The Welsh Church from Conquest to Reformation* (Cardiff: University of Wales Press, 1976) 490–491.
12. Samuel Lewis, *Topographical Dictionary of Wales*, vol. 1 (London: Lewis, 1833) 389.
13. Nancy Edwards and Tristan Gray Hulse, "A Fragment of a Reliquary Casket from Guytherin, North Wales" *Journal of the Society of Antiquaries of London* 72 (1992) 92.
14. Janet Bord, "St. Winefride's Well, Holywell, Clwyd" *Folklore* 105 (1994) 100. See also Edwards and Hulse, 91–100.
15. Giraldus Cambrensis, "Itinerary through Wales," translated by

Sir Richard Colt Hoare in *The Historical Works of Giraldus Cambrensis*, edited by Thomas Wright (London: H.G. Bohn, 1863; rpt. New York: AMS Press, 1968) 457.

16. Francis Jones, *The Holy Wells of Wales* (Cardiff: University of Wales Press, 1992) 49.

17. *The Victoria County History of Shropshire*, 2: 33.

18. Adam of Usk, *The Chronicle of Adam Usk (1377–1430)*, edited and translated by C. Given-Wilson (Oxford: Oxford University Press, 1997) 263.

19. Jones, 50.

20. *Vitæ Sanctorum Brittaniæ*, 297–301.

21. Jones, 92.

22. Williams, 495.

23. *Flintshire Historical Review* (1919/20).

24. Williams, 354–355.

25. Jones, 64–65.

26. *The Life of St. Winefride*, translated by Fr. Philip Metcalf, S.J.; edited by Rev. Herbert Thurston, S.J. (London, 1922) 100–114.

www.ingramcontent.com/pod-product-compliance
Lightning Source LLC
Chambersburg PA
CBHW072158160426
43197CB00012B/2430